D1186573

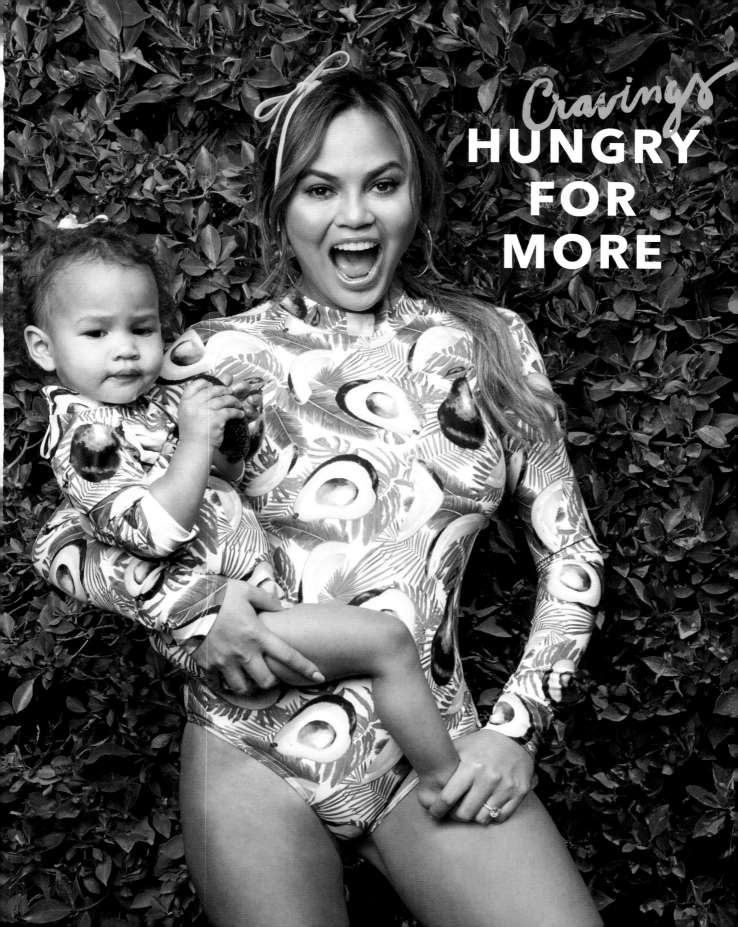

Cravings

HUNGRY
FOR
MORE

Cravings

HUNGRY
FOR MORE

CHRISSY TEIGEN

MICHAEL JOSEPH
an imprint of
PENGUIN BOOKS

CONTENTS

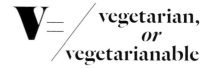

V= / vegetarian, or vegetarianable

SNACKS
95

**CRISPY COCONUT
CHICKEN GOUJONS**
with Pineapple-Chilli Sauce
96

**FRIED THAI-GLAZED
CHICKEN WINGS**
99

**ONION DIP & OVEN-BAKED
POTATO CRISPS (V)**
100

CHICKEN NACHOS
with Avocado Salsa
102

**MUSHROOM & CRISPY SHALLOT
NACHOS (V)**
105

**HOLLOWED-OUT
ITALIAN SANDWICH**
106

**KING'S HAWAIIAN PULL-APART
BACON CHEESE TOASTIES (V)**
109

**PEANUT BUTTER PRETZEL
GRANOLA CLUSTERS (V)**
110

FLUFFY CORN DOGS
113

POTATOES
& THEIR
FRIENDS
114

CRISPY POTATO SMASHIES (V)
116

CRISPY BUFFALO SMASHIES (V)
119

**CRISPY-COATED OVEN-ROASTED
SWEET POTATO WEDGES (V)**
120

TWO-TONE POTATO GRATIN (V)
123

SALT-&-VINEGAR BAKED CHIPS (V)
124

TATERS, SHROOMS & PEAS
with Parmesan Cream (V)
127

PEPPER'S GRIDDLED AUBERGINE
with Crispy Shallots
128

GOLDEN ONION RICE PILAF (V)
131

**SPICY HONEY-BUTTER
CARROT COINS (V)**
133

**JALAPEÑO-CHEDDAR
CORN PUDDING (V)**
134

**SHEET PAN CREAM & THYME
ROASTED ONIONS (V)**
137

**SWEET & SAVOURY HAM HOCK
BAKED BEANS**
138

SAUTÉED SPICY ASPARAGUS (V)
139

**KUNG PAO ROASTED
BROCCOLI**
141

**GARLICKY CAULIFLOWER
'RICE' (V)**
142

THAI MOM
144

TOM YUM NOODLES
146

**PAD THAI CARBONARA
(BACON & EGG
PAD THAI SPAGHETTI)**
148

PORK GLASS NOODLE SALAD
150

**KHAO TOD
(CRISPY RICE SALAD)**
with Fried Eggs (V)
152

THAI FISHCAKES
with Spicy Peanut Sauce
157

CRAB FRIED RICE
158

PORK LARB
161

THAI SEARED TUNA SALAD
164

RED CHICKEN CURRY
167

THAI SOY-GARLIC FRIED RIBS
168

PEPPER'S SPRING ROLLS
173

INTRODUCTION

Welcome to my second cookbook . . . so glad you came!

Two and half years have passed since *Cravings* hit the shelves, and the most popular question I got during the entire process of writing book two was 'So what's the theeeeeeme of the next one??' My first reaction was, 'More of the same, OK??' because honestly, I'm not really into gimmick books like *500-Calorie, Three-Ingredient Meals in Under Ten Minutes*. I want lifetime books, books that sit on my shelf for years and years and years with sticky pages and balsamic fingerprints.

But the truth is, this book isn't a carbon copy of the first one at all. A lot has happened over that time – you could even say I've . . . grown up a little? I got to travel and taste more things around the world, and this book has some recipes with brighter flavours and maybe *slightly* less cheese and gravy and . . . ham than *Cravings*. (Not that there's anything wrong with those things! It's just that I realized that it's also nice to eat really well, even indulgently, without a food-coma nap.)

Speaking of sleep (hey, I'm a newish mom and every new mom will tell you sleep is literally the only thing you think about), I have to tell you that I barely slept a wink between the time the first book was sent off to the printer and the day it went on sale in February 2016. I had toothpick-eyes nightly, wondering, *Would you buy my book? Would you make my food? Would you like it? Would you get food poisoning or drunk from a bread pudding loaded with booze? Were there any errors? OH MY GOD, did I write to use salt when I meant sugar?? Would I PUBLISH MY OWN PHONE NUMBER ON MY DOG'S COLLAR IN A PHOTO?* (YES.)

And then your tweets and posts and cooking parties started – there were even people who made EVERY recipe and documented it – and I swear this meant *everything* to me, more than any article or review or annoying think-piece interview about whether a model could actually cook.

Yes, I *can* cook because ANYONE can, and that was the whole entire point of *Cravings* in the first place. You proved my theory and then some, and then some, and then some more – all the way to the top of the *New York Times* bestseller list!

A lot has changed since then, obviously – we've got Luna, another bebé on the way (by the time this book comes out this boy-child will have also arrived). We moved. And I got really, really sick. Postpartum depression really kicked me in the ass, and it took me a while to get strong again, to feel good, to get off the couch and, quite frankly, to have an appetite for anything but a pillow and blanket. But in those dark times, I became strictly a couch-sleeper, keeping a dressing gown in my pantry so I wouldn't have to go upstairs to change. And John slept on that couch with me every. single. night.

One of the ways I knew I was healing was that I found my way back into the kitchen, at first slowly, and maybe just to watch my mom put together something simple in the hopes that I might take a few bites. It sounds like a cliché, but starting to cook again really helped me get back on my feet and get back into normal life. So this book is filled with food that served as landmarks in my road map to something resembling normality (or as normal as a crazy life like mine can be).

Cooking has always been my safe haven, even when things around me are changing at warp speed. So I hope this book is as stabilizing and filling a force in your life as the making of it was for me. The good part is, no matter how you feel, I know you'll be sure to let me know! I wouldn't have it any other way.

XOXOXO,
Chrissy

TWO THINGS BEFORE YOU START COOKING

OK, so in some cookbooks they start you off with sixteen pages of rules – you *have* to cut your herbs with a razor blade to get the right flavour, *obviously* – but we made sure you can dive right in and start cooking without any of that in this book. WELL, EXCEPT. There are two things you NEED to know.

1. **SALT**. I loves it. But I don't loves too much of it, so: When I call for 'kosher salt' in these recipes, I used Diamond Crystal brand. Other brands, like Morton's, are much saltier, so use less salt – like, a full third less. They're easily available online.

2. **GRATED PARMESAN**, which is like the salt of the cheese world. I *also* loves me my Parm Parm Parm Parm Parm. When I say 'finely grated', I mean to grate it on a Microplane – they're amazing little graters and they make the lightest shavings; weigh it after it's been grated. (For other grated or shredded cheeses in these recipes, just use the big holes on a box grater.)

BREAKFAST & BRUNCH

FRENCH TOAST
with Whipped Honey Ricotta Topping

When I was growing up, French toast was one of the handful of non-Thai things my mom would make AND actually eat. We, of course, loved us some sliced bread at the time but I hiiiiiighly recommend going the extra mile and getting a big loaf of brioche. Make your slices nice and thick to absorb all the eggy goodness. You are going to freak out when you press your fork into it for the first bite and you see how perfectly soft and fluffy and ooey gooey this monster is.

Do you remember the rum-soaked, salty-cornflake-topped French toast casserole from *Cravings*?? The one you "accidentally" spilled extra booze into and made with all your nonjudgmental friends? The one you tagged me in thousands of awesome Instagram posts with? This is its not-so-naughty neighbor.

SERVES 6
ACTIVE TIME / 15 MIN
TOTAL TIME / 30 MIN

FOR THE WHIPPED RICOTTA TOPPING

- **500 g whole-milk ricotta cheese**
- **6 tablespoons double cream**
- **4 tbsp honey**
- **½ teaspoon vanilla extract**
- **¼ teaspoon ground cinnamon**

FOR THE HONEY BUTTER SYRUP

- **4 tbsp honey**
- **4 tablespoons butter**
- **¼ teaspoon vanilla extract**
- **Kosher salt**

FOR THE FRENCH TOAST

- **1 (30-cm) loaf day-old brioche**
- **4 eggs**
- **435 ml whole milk**
- **60 ml cream double or single**
- **1 teaspoon vanilla extract**
- **Kosher salt**
- **Dash of grated nutmeg**
- **Butter, for the pan**

MAKE THE WHIPPED RICOTTA TOPPING In a large bowl, combine the ricotta, cream, honey, vanilla and cinnamon and whisk until everything fluffs up a bit, 30 seconds to 1 minute. Cover and chill.

MAKE THE HONEY BUTTER SYRUP In a small saucepan, combine the honey, butter, vanilla and a few pinches of salt and heat over low heat until the mixture begins to bubble. Remove from the heat. Stir to recombine, if necessary, and cover to keep warm.

MAKE THE FRENCH TOAST Cut the bread into slices 2 inches thick. In a 20-cm square baking dish, whisk the eggs, milk, cream, vanilla, a few pinches of salt and nutmeg. Dip each piece of bread in the egg mixture for 10 seconds per side if you want lighter, fluffier French toast, or 20 to 30 seconds per side for creamier, more custardy and undercooked-in-a-good-way centres. Put the slices of bread on a baking sheet to hold.

Heat a large frying pan or griddle over medium-low heat. Grease the pan generously with butter and add as many slices of bread as will fit comfortably in one layer. Cook until the bread is golden and toasty, about 5 minutes per side. Repeat with remaining bread, greasing the pan again between batches.

Divide the French toast among plates, dollop with ricotta, and drizzle with syrup.

Blueberry Cream Cheese
PANCAKES

I am no stranger to the chain restaurant. I tried, and failed, to work at Red Robin just for access to their steak fries. I was, for a moment, a Hooter Girl hostess. I remember running food for one of the other girls (A HUGE HOSTESS NO-NO IN A TIP-BASED RESTAURANT) and almost getting smacked in the face with a pair of double G's. I still go to Applebee's for riblets. And I am not the biggest fan of desserts, EXCEPT for the sour cream blueberry pie at Marie Callender's. And I haaaaate sour cream. But I do love its slightly sweeter twin sister, cream cheese.

These pancakes remind me sooooo much of that pie behind that glass. Little bombs of cream cheese melt into the batter as it oozes across your griddle. The little bit of vinegar makes the pancakes puff, and it's a trick you should keep to yourself. Everyone will think only you can make pancakes this fluffy.

SERVES 6
ACTIVE TIME / 15 MIN
TOTAL TIME / 40 MIN

225 g full-fat cream cheese or mascarpone (not the tub of spread), cold

250 g plain flour

5 tablespoons sugar

2 teaspoons baking powder

1 teaspoon baking soda

¼ teaspoon kosher salt

585 ml buttermilk

2 eggs

110 g butter, melted and slightly cooled

¼ teaspoon distilled white vinegar

110 g juicy blueberries, plus more for serving

Butter and pancake syrup (Aunt Jemima preferred! But pure maple if you insist), for serving

3 digestive biscuits, crushed into crumbs

Cut the cream cheese into 5-mm cubes (see Note) and put it in the freezer while you start the batter.

In a large bowl, whisk together the flour, sugar, baking powder, baking soda and salt. In a separate bowl, whisk together the buttermilk, eggs, half the butter, and vinegar. Stir the wet ingredients into the flour mixture. Let the batter sit around for 5 minutes, then stir in the cream cheese cubes.

Heat a griddle or cast-iron frying pan over medium-high heat. Reduce the heat to medium, brush the griddle with some of the remaining melted butter, and use a ladle (75 ml) to measure the batter on to the griddle. Dot each pancake with 1 tablespoon of the blueberries and cook until tiny bubbles push up through the pancakes and the edges are lacy and brown, 1 to 2 minutes. Flip and cook until the underside is cooked and lacy, another 1 to 2 minutes. Continue cooking the pancakes, brushing the griddle with more melted butter between batches.

Stack 2 or 3 pancakes on each plate, dot with butter, drizzle with syrup, and sprinkle with biscuit crumbs and blueberries.

Note / *CREAM CHEESE BOMBS*

When spread, cream cheese is a pleasant blanket for bread. But if you leave it in cubes, it holds its shape and contains a sour creaminess that adds a ton of flavour to recipes like this one and the Everything Bagel Cream Cheese Breakfast

Note / THE BEST WAY TO COOK BACON

If you're cooking more than just a few slices of bacon, this is *the best way to do it:* Preheat the oven to 375°F/190°C. Lay the bacon (say, 12 slices) out on a rimmed baking sheet so the slices don't overlap. Roast until crisp, 12 to 15 minutes.

Crispy Parmesan
WAFFLE BREAKFAST

Adding Parm to these waffles crisps up the outside, forming a light shell of cheese (because . . . just listen to how that sounds: 'a light shell of cheese'). The spicy maple tastes like it came out of some weird Pepper Thai dream – just warm some syrup with some butter and a few little red hotties and your syrup becomes a spicy-sweet Thai condiment weapon.

SERVES 4
ACTIVE TIME / 10 MIN
TOTAL TIME / 30 MIN

125 g plain flour

1 teaspoon baking powder

½ teaspoon baking soda

1 teaspoon freshly ground black pepper, plus more for sprinkling

½ teaspoon kosher salt

310 ml buttermilk

3 tablespoons butter, melted, plus more for brushing the waffle maker

1 egg

120 g finely grated Parmigiano-Reggiano cheese, plus a little more for sprinkling

FOR SERVING

4 eggs, cooked how you like them

8 slices bacon, cooked (optional; see Note)

Maple syrup or Spicy Buttery Maple Syrup (recipe follows)

Preheat the oven to warm, or as low as it will go.

In a large bowl, whisk together the flour, baking powder, baking soda, pepper and salt. In another bowl, whisk together the buttermilk, melted butter and egg until incorporated. Add the wet ingredients to the flour mixture and whisk until just incorporated (a few lumps are OK), then whisk in the Parm.

Heat a standard waffle iron, brush with some melted butter, and make the waffles using between 175 and 200 ml batter per batch. Cook according to the waffle iron's directions or until the top and bottom are crisp and deep brown, 5 to 6 minutes. Remove the waffle from the iron (you may have to pick at it from one of the ends with a fork, but, uh, don't electrocute yourself). Put the waffle on a baking sheet in the oven to keep warm while you cook the remaining waffles.

Arrange a waffle on a plate and top with an egg and 2 slices of bacon, if using. Drizzle with syrup and sprinkle with a little more Parm and pepper.

Spicy Buttery Maple Syrup

MAKES 250 ml
ACTIVE TIME / 1 MIN
TOTAL TIME / 5 MIN

110 g butter

175 ml maple syrup

1 teaspoon chilli flakes

1 teaspoon kosher salt

In a small saucepan, melt the butter over medium-low heat. Add the maple syrup, chilli flakes and salt. Bring to a simmer to meld the flavours, then remove from the heat. Serve warm immediately, or let come to room temperature to develop more flavour. Rewarm over low heat and stir to recombine if you need to before serving.

Buttermilk-Chive
BISCUIT
BREAKFAST
SANDWICHES

SERVES 4 WITH EXTRA BISCUITS
ACTIVE TIME / 35 MIN
TOTAL TIME / 1 HR

I'm not above rolling up to the drive-thru for a perfectly buttery biscuit breakfast sammie. (OK, let's be honest, ordering from Just Eat, because why leave the house really?) But homemade? I mean, *c'mon*. Making bread is scarier for me than the people in *Winter's Bone* or a life without Andy Cohen, but these really are doable (if you don't mind sticky fingers and a little anxiety before they rise and puff up – as they do every time). Anyway, once you have the biscuits made, you're good: You slow-scramble some creamy, creamy eggs and pile them on top of the biscuit with unsmoked back bacon, aka Canadian bacon, which, like Canada in general, is really nice and less offensive than its American counterpart.

2 tablespoons olive oil

1 large onion, thinly sliced

2 tablespoons butter, plus softened butter for buttering the biscuits

½ teaspoon kosher salt

¼ teaspoon freshly ground black pepper

60 g rocket

4 slices unsmoked back bacon (optional)

4 Buttermilk-Chive Biscuits (recipe follows)

4 eggs, slow-scrambled (see Tip)

In a large frying pan, heat the oil over medium heat. Add the onion and cook, stirring, until the onion reduces in size, about 10 minutes. Reduce the heat to medium-low, add the 2 tablespoons butter, the salt and pepper, and cook, stirring, until the onion is soft and caramelized, another 12 to 15 minutes. Add the rocket one handful at a time and cook, stirring, after each addition, until the rocket is wilted, about 1 minute. Transfer the mixture to a bowl and cover to keep warm.

Add the bacon, if using, to the pan and cook until browned, 1 to 2 minutes per side.

Split the biscuits, butter generously, and top one side of each biscuit with a slice of bacon and some of the eggs, and the other side with the onion-rocket mixture. Serve open-faced or close up and eat like a sandwich.

Tip / *SLOW-SCRAMBLING EGGS*

My favourite way to scramble eggs is, for every 4 eggs, whisk in 2½ tablespoons cream, and salt and pepper to taste. In a nonstick frying pan, heat 1 tablespoon butter and 1 tablespoon olive oil over low (YES, I SAID LOW) heat. When the butter is melted, pour in the eggs and stir with a silicone spatula *foreverrrrrr* (or like 4 to 6 minutes, or more like 12 to 14 minutes if you're cooking a whole dozen, or like 30 if your stove can go that low and if you can stand it), until the eggs are just cooked: super soft and creamy and custardy. If you've never done it this way, do it and thank me on Insta.

Buttermilk-Chive Biscuits

MAKES 6
ACTIVE TIME / 20 MIN
TOTAL TIME / 50 MIN

420 g plain flour, plus more for dusting

4 teaspoons baking powder

1 teaspoon baking soda

1 teaspoon kosher salt

110 g cold butter

250 ml buttermilk, or a little more if necessary, plus more for brushing

2 tablespoons chopped chives

Preheat the oven to 450°F/230°C.

In a medium bowl, whisk together the flour, baking powder, baking soda and salt and throw it in the freezer. Cut the cold butter into cubes and put it in the freezer. Measure out the buttermilk and keep it chillin' in the fridge. Chill everything for at least 15 minutes.

Dump the flour mixture into a food processor and pulse a couple of times. Add the butter to the processor and pulse until the butter is mixed in but still in pea-size pieces, 7 or 8 pulses. Drizzle the buttermilk over the mixture, add the chives, and pulse some more, *just until* the mixture forms a loose, shaggy dough, 10 to 15 pulses, adding more buttermilk by the tablespoon if necessary to get it to form a dough. (When in doubt, underpulse! That is not actually a word! But you understand.)

Dust a work surface with flour. Turn the dough out on to it. Sprinkle your hands with flour and press the dough into a 15 × 20 cm rectangle. Really try to gently pat the dough and don't drag your hands through it; this helps keep it tender and fluffy when baked. It's not magic, it's science.

Fold the dough in half, then fold it in half again in the other direction, until you have a 7.5 × 12.5 cm rectangle. Re-flour your hands and pat the dough into a 15 × 18 mm rectangle about 2.5 cm thick. Using the sharpest knife you have, cut the dough into six 7.5 cm squares; try not to drag the knife too much and just make a sharp cut; this will help the biscuits rise more.

Transfer the biscuits to an ungreased baking sheet, brush with buttermilk, and bake until the tops are golden and the biscuits have risen and are fluffy, 12 to 13 minutes. Serve warm.

Eat leftover biscuits within a couple of days (toasting helps). Or wrap the biscuits tightly in plastic wrap and keep frozen for up to 3 months. Thaw before toasting.

Black Bean & Mushroom
ENCHILADA CASSEROLE

I have no reason behind this delicious beast of a dish aside from the fact that I am pregnant (again) as I write this and being pregnant means I basically eat so much all day that I have started to combine cravings. I love burritos. I love mushrooms. I love beans. I love enchiladas so I put them all together. And I LOVE eating between conventional food-eating times, so I love brunch. This has to be one of the most group-friendly brunch dishes around. Please have it with a spicy margarita or Bloody Mary, I beg you. Do it for me, because I can't. Doctors these days.

SERVES 6
ACTIVE TIME / 40 MIN
TOTAL TIME / 1 HR 15 MIN

3 tablespoons vegetable oil, plus more for the baking dish and frying the eggs

1 large onion, chopped

2 tablespoons minced garlic

335 g white mushrooms, trimmed and thinly sliced

1 large or 2 medium jalapeño peppers, seeded and diced

1½ teaspoons kosher salt

½ teaspoon freshly ground black pepper

8 g chopped fresh coriander, plus more for garnish

1 teaspoon ground cumin

1 400 g can black beans, drained and rinsed

60 ml chicken stock or water

8 (20-cm) flour tortillas

Tomatillo Sauce (recipe follows)

220 g shredded Mexican blend cheese

6 eggs

1 avocado, sliced, for serving

Preheat the oven to 350°F/175°C.

In a large frying pan, heat the 3 tablespoons oil over medium heat. Add the onion and cook, stirring, until soft and lightly golden but not too dark, about 9 minutes. Add the garlic and cook 1 minute. Add the mushrooms, jalapeños, salt and black pepper. Crank up the heat to medium-high and cook, stirring, until the mushrooms release their water and soften, about 7 minutes. Add the coriander, cumin, black beans, and stock and cook, stirring gently, until hot, about 3 minutes.

Grease a 25 × 30-cm baking dish with vegetable oil. Spoon an eighth of the bean filling into a tortilla, roll it up into a log (you don't have to fold the sides in), and place it seam-side down in the dish. (This is a fun, very neat thing to do with a baby human crawling around on the work surface.) Repeat with the remaining filling and tortillas, lining them up to fill the dish. Pour 250 ml of the tomatillo sauce over the rolled tortillas, leaving a few spots in the middle and at the ends so the tortillas are exposed, then sprinkle the cheese on top and bake until the cheese is bubbling and the edges are crisped, 25 to 30 minutes.

About 5 minutes before the casserole is done, fry the eggs however you like them, so they're ready when the casserole comes out.

Cut the casserole into 6 squares, divide among plates, and top each serving with an egg and some avocado slices. Garnish with coriander. Pass the extra tomatillo sauce at the table.

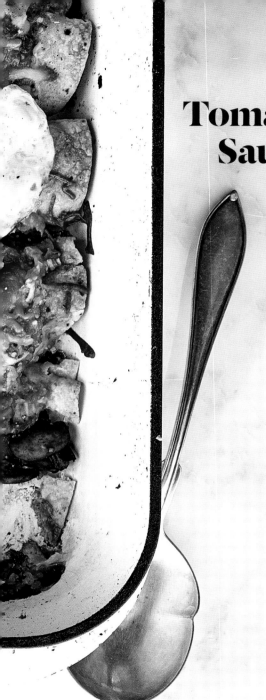

Tomatillo Sauce

675 g tomatillos, husks removed and rinsed, or 1 (28-ounce) can whole tomatillos, well drained

1 medium onion, cut into 1-inch wedges

5 large cloves garlic (I mean large! Or they might burn), unpeeled

2 large or 3 medium jalapeño peppers, halved and seeded

1 tablespoon vegetable oil

1 teaspoon kosher salt

½ teaspoon freshly ground black pepper

Preheat the grill to medium. Line the grill pan with foil.

In a large bowl, toss together the tomatillos, onion, garlic, jalapeños, oil, salt, and pepper. Dump it all on to the lined grill pan and spread everything out into one layer. Grill until the tomatillos slump and the jalapeños and onion wedges are charred, about 15 minutes (start checking after 10 minutes).

Remove from the grill, cool slightly, and peel the garlic. Process everything in a food processor or blender until smooth.

MAKES 750 ml
ACTIVE TIME / 15 MIN
TOTAL TIME / 30 MIN

Note

Tomatillos are a staple of Mexican cuisine. The tins are available online in the UK or you could try a combination of green tomatoes and green peppers.

Pepper's Garlicky Bacon
SCRAMBLE

My mom has been making these eggs my entire life because we are never, ever without these ingredients. I LIVED on them when I was pregnant. Luna is basically made of these greasy, garlicky eggs. The recipe varies depending on what's in the fridge or what kind of laziness level my mom is at, but some things always remain the same: bacon, fresh coriander, garlic and shallots. They go together like Sonny and Cher and two other people that also go together to make that analogy work. It's been a long time since I've written, OK, give me a f*cking break.

SERVES 2
ACTIVE TIME / 5 MIN
TOTAL TIME / 15 MIN

4 eggs

2 tablespoons whole milk

2 thick-cut or 3 regular slices bacon, finely diced

1 small shallot, finely diced, or 3 tablespoons finely diced onion

1 small clove garlic, finely minced

2 tablespoons picked fresh coriander leaves

Kosher salt and freshly ground black pepper

Sliced avocado and buttered toast, for serving

In a small bowl, whisk together the eggs and milk. In a 20-or 22-cm nonstick frying pan or super well-seasoned cast-iron pan, cook the bacon over medium heat until lightly crisped and the fat has rendered (not as burny-crisp as regular bacon), 5 to 6 minutes. Add the shallot and garlic and cook until softened, about 2 minutes. Reduce the heat to low, add the eggs, coriander and a good sprinkle of salt and pepper, and cook, pushing the eggs around occasionally, until large curds form and the eggs are no longer wet and shiny, about 2 minutes. Transfer the eggs to a plate and serve with avocado slices and buttered toast.

AVOCADO with TOASTY CRUMBS

Let's be real. Avocado toast has been done every which way and 100 per cent of those ways are freaking awesome. I can't believe I spent half my life hating avocados. Now, as a form of self-punishment, I will devote the rest of my life to getting other avocado haters to come to Jesus. This is usually by way of my (controversial) cheddar cheese guacamole from my first book, but it now comes in the form of this . . . *reverse* avocado toast: perfect avocado halves showered with a ton of toasty bread crumbs with a cayenne kick.

SERVES 2
ACTIVE TIME / 10 MIN
TOTAL TIME / 15 MIN

2 slices white bread (crusts are OK)

2 tablespoons olive oil

Kosher salt and freshly ground black pepper

Dash of cayenne pepper

1 teaspoon finely chopped chives

1 teaspoon finely chopped fresh flat-leaf parsley

1 gorgeous, ripe avocado

2 lemon wedges

2 small radishes, thinly sliced

Tear the bread a little and put it in a food processor; process until it turns into fine crumbs, about 15 seconds. Dump the bread into a cold frying pan and add the olive oil, ¼ teaspoon salt, ¼ teaspoon black pepper, and cayenne. Turn the heat to medium-low and cook the crumbs, stirring, until toasty and crisp all the way through, about 10 minutes. Dump the crumbs into a bowl to cool (if you leave them in the pan they'll burn). Add the chives and parsley. Season to taste with salt and pepper.

Just before serving, peel the avocado (see Tip), halve it, squeeze a little lemon on to each half, season it with salt and pepper, plate it, and top it generously with the crumbs and radish slices.

Tip / HOW TO PEEL AN AVOCADO

Using a sharp knife, start at the narrow end of the avocado, run the knife all around the avocado, hitting the pit at the centre, until you've come back to where you started. Grab the avocado with both hands and twist it apart (the pit will remain in one side). Take the heel of the knife (the thickest part, just above the handle) and tap it into the pit, then twist the knife to dislodge it. Then you can either use a giant spoon to scoop the flesh out of the skin in one firm motion, or you can do this: Place the avocado halves, skin side up, on a cutting board. Using a paring knife, cut the skin (but don't cut all the way through into the flesh), working from one end to the other. Then gently peel away the skin in long strips to reveal the avocado.

Everything Bagel
Cream Cheese
BREAKFAST BAKE

I have felt for a long time that everything bagel spice is the bomb. But I've never been that into eating an entire bagel – it's just too much dough at one time. Cutting them up into pieces and baking them with sausage and eggs though . . . That, folks, is *everything*.

SERVES 8
ACTIVE TIME / 20 MIN
TOTAL TIME / 1 HR 35 MIN
(plus resting time)

450 g breakfast sausages* (optional)

2 tablespoons butter, plus more for the baking dish

1 large onion, thinly sliced

280 g frozen spinach, thawed

3 day-old everything bagels, halved and cut into big chunks

2 large tomatoes, cut into chunks

5 g chopped fresh basil

80 g finely grated Parmigiano-Reggiano cheese

135 g grated Gruyère or Swiss cheese

135 g grated cheddar cheese

2 teaspoons kosher salt

1 teaspoon freshly ground black pepper

8 eggs

500 ml milk

250 ml single cream

2 tablespoons Dijon mustard

¼ teaspoon cayenne pepper

225 g full-fat cream cheese or mascarpone, cold, cut into 14 cubes

Melt the butter in the pan over medium-low heat, then add the onion and cook, stirring occasionally, until lightly golden and translucent, about 9 minutes. While the onion is cooking, pile the thawed spinach into the centre of a big clean kitchen towel and roll up the towel. Over a bowl or the sink, twist the ends toward each other and keep twisting until you wring out as much liquid as humanly possible. (Or make someone else do this.)

Transfer the spinach to the bowl with the sausage and add the onion, bagel chunks, tomatoes, basil, Parm, two thirds each of the Gruyère and cheddar, 1 teaspoon of the salt and ½ teaspoon of the pepper. Toss it all together with your hands or a spoon. In a separate bowl, whisk together the eggs, milk, cream, mustard, cayenne, and the remaining 1 teaspoon salt and ½ teaspoon black pepper.

Grease a 22.5 × 33-cm baking dish with butter and arrange the bagel mixture in the dish. Pour the egg mixture over the top, pressing down on the bagels so they soak up the liquid. Nestle the cream cheese chunks in all around the pan (they can be peeking out). Cover and refrigerate for at least 1½ hours and up to 12 hours. (The longer you soak, the moister the inside will be.)

Preheat the oven to 400°F/200°C.

Uncover the dish and sprinkle with the remaining Gruyère and cheddar. Bake for 15 minutes, reduce the temperature to 350°F/175°C, and bake until the top is golden and the centre is set, 50 minutes to 1 hour.

Heat a large frying pan with a tight-fitting lid over medium heat. Add the sausages, if using, and cook, turning occasionally, until cooked through, about 12 minutes (or according to the directions on the package). Remove the sausages from the pan, cut into 2.5-cm lengths, place in a large bowl, and set aside.

Note

An everything bagel is, literally a bagel with every topping – onion, salt, sesame seeds and poppy seeds. Everything bagel spice has added garlic.

If you want to keep this veggie, omit the sausage, increase the butter for sautéing the onions by 1 tablespoon, and add another 150 g of thawed frozen spinach.

EGG-MOZZARELLA HAM CUPS

Oh, ham cups. You remind me so much of my early blog days. When cooking was merely a hobby and there was zero pressure to pump out the prettiest, filtered photos. No deadlines. No 'can I say this or will I get in trouble?!' Oh, those were the days.

Sharing this recipe humbles me. It's so simple. When I posted it many many years ago, it was so ugly, so dry, so overcooked, but you loved it. You BELIEVED in it. You didn't make fun of me. Instead, you flooded my comment section with tips and tricks and other fillings that could be great. That blog was our little community. I was super insecure about sharing (at the time) and REALLY insecure about sharing my love of cooking when I had soooooo little actual knowledge, just a passion for it. But you guys were so cool to me and we learned together. I think this might be the recipe that kept me going. It's the recipe that is why we are here today with this second book! That's pretty awesome. You guys are awesome.

MAKES 6
ACTIVE TIME / 10 MIN
TOTAL TIME / 25 MIN

6 thin slices ham

45 g finely diced mozzarella, or tiny mozzarella balls

80 g halved cherry tomatoes or diced tomatoes

2 tablespoons pesto (recipe follows), or store-bought

2 tablespoons fresh bread crumbs (see page 178)

Kosher salt and freshly ground black pepper

6 eggs

330 g salad leaves

Red wine vinegar

Extra-virgin olive oil

Preheat the oven to 400°F/200°C. Coat 6 cups of a standard nonstick muffin tin with cooking spray.

Tuck one thin slice of ham into each cup, trying to make as much of a cup shape as possible with the edges sticking out the top. If you've made the Croissant Bread Pudding Ham Cups (page 32) before, this step will feel a little less ridiculous because you're going to put eggs into that ham instead of bread pudding. That's just how it works. I don't know why.

In a bowl, combine the mozzarella, tomatoes, pesto and bread crumbs. Season to taste with salt and pepper and divide the mixture among the ham cups. Carefully crack an egg into each cup. Bake until the tomato juices are lightly bubbling and the whites are set, about 15 minutes.

In a large bowl, toss the leaves with salt, pepper, vinegar and oil to taste to make a simple salad. Let the ham cups cool slightly, then unmold them by slipping a knife under the cups and gently transferring them to a plate. Serve the ham cups with the salad on the side.

Pesto

MAKES ABOUT 250 ml
ACTIVE TIME / 5 MIN
TOTAL TIME / 5 MIN

50 g fresh basil leaves

45 g pine nuts

3 garlic cloves, minced

80 g finely grated Parmigiano-Reggiano cheese

125 ml extra-virgin olive oil

Salt and freshly ground black pepper

Pulse the basil, pine nuts, garlic and Parm in a food processor 15 times. Turn on the processor and add the oil in a slow, small stream. Scrape down the sides of the bowl if necessary. Season with salt and pepper to taste.

CROISSANT BREAD PUDDING HAM CUPS

Soooo if you read my little ham cup saga (see page 31), you know I am emotionally committed to ham cups because you've given me so much love and so many ideas for them. Well, then, here's another one.

(see page 31)

MAKES 6
ACTIVE TIME / 10 MIN
TOTAL TIME / 40 MIN

6 thin slices ham

3 eggs

185 ml single cream

50 g granulated sugar

1½ teaspoons vanilla extract

Kosher salt

1 large or 2 medium day-old croissants

Demerara sugar, for sprinkling

Berries, for serving (optional)

Preheat the oven to 400°F/200°C. Coat 6 cups of a standard nonstick muffin tin with cooking spray.

Tuck one thin slice of ham into each cup, trying to make as much of a cup shape as possible with the edges sticking out the top. You're going to feel ridiculous doing this. It's OK. Life is ridiculous.

In a bowl, whisk together the eggs and cream, then add the granulated sugar, vanilla and a dash of salt.

Tear the croissant into 5-cm pieces. Throw the pieces into the egg mixture, toss to coat, and let sit 15 minutes.

Fill the ham cups with the croissant mixture and sprinkle each one with Demerara sugar. Bake until the tops are golden and crusty, about 15 minutes. Let them cool slightly, then unmold them by slipping a knife under the cups and gently transferring them to a plate. Serve with berries, if desired.

CHEESY POLENTA
with Mushrooms

I present to you a sexy little breakfast (or lunch or dinner, really) dish that will have people scratching their heads: *She made that?* But little do they know that polenta is the Quaker's Porridge Oats of the corn world; you just add water and a bunch of really good stuff (butter, cream and cheese) and stir, stir, stir until it drinks it all up and turns into a rich and creamy resting place for my little sliced mushroom and sunny egg babies before they find their permanent home in my belly. So yes, *you made that*. Or at least you will.

SERVES 4
ACTIVE TIME / 30 MIN
TOTAL TIME / 30 MIN

FOR THE POLENTA
140 g dry polenta

2 teaspoons kosher salt

170 ml double cream, slightly warmed

60 g finely grated Parmigiano-Reggiano cheese, plus more for finishing

65 g shredded mozzarella cheese

2 tablespoons butter

½ teaspoon freshly ground black pepper

FOR THE MUSHROOMS
2 tablespoons olive oil

3 cloves garlic, thinly sliced

250 g white mushrooms, sliced

Splash of chicken stock or water

1 tablespoon butter

2 tablespoons double cream

1 teaspoon chopped fresh thyme, plus more for garnish

Kosher salt and freshly ground black pepper

FOR SERVING
4 eggs, cooked sunny-side up

MAKE THE POLENTA In a medium saucepan, bring 750 ml water to a boil over medium-high heat. Stir in the polenta and 1 teaspoon of the salt, reduce the heat to medium-low and simmer, stirring often, until the mixture thickens and bubbles like molten lava, about 20 minutes.

Stir in the cream, Parm, mozzarella, butter, remaining 1 teaspoon salt, and the pepper, stirring until the polenta has loosened slightly and everything is melted and incorporated. Turn off the heat and cover the pot to keep warm while you cook the mushrooms.

MEANWHILE, MAKE THE MUSHROOMS In the largest frying pan you have, heat the oil over medium heat. Add the garlic and cook until fragrant but not too brown, about 1 minute. Add the mushrooms and cook, stirring, until the mushrooms release their water but there is still water in the pan (this is like an instant mushroom stock) and the mushrooms are well on their way to silky and tender, about 6 minutes. Splash in the chicken stock and cook, stirring, for 1 minute. Stir in the butter, cream and thyme, season with plenty of salt and pepper, and cook until everything is slightly thickened, about 1 minute.

Divide the polenta among wide, shallow bowls, top each bowl with some of the mushrooms and a sunny-side-up egg, and garnish with thyme.

Fluffy **YORKSHIRE PUDS** with Melted Brie & Blackberry Jam

As these beautiful weirdos bake, they puff their eggy selves up with tons of hot air before developing a gorgeous, dark brown shell you gotta eat fast to enjoy at 100 per cent. But first: Break them open (watch out for that burst of hot steam!) and dollop in jam you make yourself in a flash (or swap in store-bought if you got stuck watching the season finale of *Below Deck*) and a wedge of molten Brie cheese.

MAKES 12
ACTIVE TIME / 10 MIN
TOTAL TIME / 1 HR
(includes preheating oven)

- **420 ml milk**
- **4 eggs, beaten**
- **2 tablespoons butter, melted, plus more for the muffin tin**
- **220g plain flour**
- **½ teaspoon salt**
- **6 ounces Brie cheese, rind removed**
- **Blackberry Jam (recipe follows), or any jam you like**

Preheat the oven to 425°F/220°C. Generously butter 12 cups of a standard muffin tin.

Place the milk in a large microwave-safe bowl and warm in the microwave just to get the chill off of it, about 1 minute. Whisk in the eggs, 2 tablespoons melted butter, flour and salt until smooth. Place the muffin tin in the oven to preheat for 2 to 3 minutes (if you go much more, the butter could start to smoke or burn).

Remove the pan from the oven and, working fasssssst (but don't burn yourself!), add about 60 ml batter to each muffin cup. Bake until puffed and dark golden (they will be in no way symmetrical and will have puffed out in all sorts of directions), 20 to 25 minutes.

During the last minute of cooking, place the Brie in a microwave-safe bowl and microwave until melted, about 30 seconds.

Remove the puds from the oven and immediately poke the tops open and drop some of the melted Brie inside each popover. Top with a dollop of jam.

Blackberry Jam

MAKES 400 g
ACTIVE TIME / 5 MIN
TOTAL TIME / 25 MIN

- **330 g blackberries**
- **150 g sugar**
- **3 tablespoons lemon juice**
- **½ teaspoon finely grated lemon zest**

In a smallish, wide saucepan, combine the blackberries, sugar and 2 tablespoons of the lemon juice. Bring to a boil over medium-high heat, reduce the heat, and cook at a simmer, stirring often and mashing the fruit (use a potato masher if you've got one!), until the mixture has thickened and is glossy, about 20 minutes. Remove from the heat and stir in the remaining 1 tablespoon lemon juice and the zest. (It may look like the jam loosens too much when the lemon juice is added, but it firms back up as it cools so don't sweat it.) You can keep it in a jar in the fridge for a couple weeks.

Cheesy Spicy
BREAKFAST HASH

Wow. These potatoes are good. Like, breakfast-for-dinner, right-out-of-the-pan, utensils-optional good. Especially since they are made with two of my personal fave major food groups: spuds and cheese. If you use Yukons (the ones that are waxier and a little more golden inside 1–1 available online in the UK), they'll be buttery AF (that's just how Yukons taste). Idahos (or russets) have that powdery fluffy All-American thing going on. A perfect equivalent in the UK is the King Edward. You say potato, I say potahtoe.

SERVES 4
ACTIVE TIME / 20 MIN
TOTAL TIME / 40 MIN

550 g potatoes, unpeeled, cut into ½-inch dice

60 ml vegetable oil

1 large onion, cut into ½-inch (1-cm) dice

6 cloves garlic, coarsely chopped

1 large green pepper, seeded and diced

2 jalapeño peppers, diced (take the seeds out first if you don't get excited by a lot of spice)

Kosher salt

½ teaspoon freshly ground black pepper

1 teaspoon paprika

125 ml vegetable or chicken stock (or water)

90 g grated cheddar cheese

6 eggs, cooked sunny-side up, for serving

Hot sauce, for serving

In a microwave-safe bowl, combine the potatoes and 1 inch (2 cm) of water. Cover and cook on high until the potatoes are partially cooked, 5 to 6 minutes. Drain the potatoes and set aside.

Heat the oil in a large cast-iron frying pan over medium-high heat until shimmering-hot. Add the onion, garlic, pepper and jalapeños and cook, stirring occasionally, until the onion is translucent and the peppers are softened, about 8 minutes.

Reduce the heat to medium, then stir in the potatoes, 1 teaspoon salt, the black pepper and paprika. Pour the stock into the pan and cook, stirring only once in a while, until the potatoes are cooked, the whole mess is golden and crispy things happen, about 15 minutes.

Taste and add more salt if it's not already super delicious. Sprinkle with the cheese, cover, and cook until the cheese is melted, another 3 to 4 minutes. Serve with the eggs and hot sauce, of course.

Salted Maple
GRANOLA

Granola is such a negative word. Maybe it's from growing up in the Pacific Northwest, where we described anyone boring AF as 'granola'. But in my old age, I would now take being called granola as a compliment. I love a good 'fridge sh*t' dish – some divine recipe made from whatever it is you've got stuffed in the crannies of your refrigerator. Granola is the ultimate pantry sh*t recipe. Once you've got the base down, check the marijuana laws of your homeland, do or do not smoke a j and raid your pantry for your favourite flavours and Go. To. Town. I loves me some toasty, salty oats, ohhhhhhh baby. Or salty, toasty oats with dried sour cherries and coconut flakes ughhhhhhh or salty, toasty oats paired with a peanut butter pretzel sitch, or toasty, salty oats tossed with shredded mozzarella and diced Peperami*. ENDLESS POSSIBILITIES.

MAKES ABOUT 750 g
ACTIVE TIME / 10 MIN
TOTAL TIME / 40 MIN

225 g old-fashioned rolled oats

50 g unsweetened finely shredded coconut

50 g chopped pecans

50 g sliced almonds

30 g sunflower seeds

125 ml vegetable oil or melted coconut oil

110 g maple syrup

130 g (packed) light brown sugar

2 teaspoons vanilla extract

2½ teaspoons kosher salt

160 g chopped dried cherries (the sourer the better)

Preheat the oven to 350°F/175°C. Line a large, rimmed baking sheet with parchment paper.

In a large bowl, combine the oats, coconut, pecans, almonds and sunflower seeds. In a small bowl, whisk together the oil, maple syrup, brown sugar, vanilla and salt. Add to the oat mixture and toss together. Spread the granola on the baking sheet and bake until golden brown, stirring occasionally, 25 to 30 minutes (the edges will get a nice, dark brown colour, but if you think the nuts are entering Burnville, pull it). Remove from the oven, cool completely and stir in the cherries. Granola keeps, stored in an airtight container, for up to 2 weeks.

 Do not actually do this. The possibilities ended right before this suggestion. Trust me on this.

SOUPS

Lazy Prawn & Pork
'WONTON' SOUP

This soup isn't lazy, I am – which is why, instead of lovingly wrapping individual wontons I'm just gonna go ahead and cook a couple of big surf-and-turf meatballs in mushroom broth, and take the extra wrappers from Mom's spring roll production and slice them into the soup like noodles. Instead of four big meatballs, you *could* hand-roll them into more, smaller balls, but again, please refer back to the first word in this recipe's name.

SERVES 4
ACTIVE TIME / 15 MIN*
TOTAL TIME / 35 MIN

FOR THE MEATBALLS

225 g ground pork

225 g peeled and deveined prawns, tails removed, finely chopped

30 g fresh bread crumbs (see page 178)

1 tablespoon minced garlic (2 to 3 cloves)

1 tablespoon finely minced fresh ginger (from a 2-cm piece)

25 g sliced spring onions, plus more for garnish

4 g finely chopped fresh coriander, plus more for garnish

2½ teaspoons chopped fresh jalapeño peppers, or to taste, plus thinly sliced rounds for garnish

½ teaspoon kosher salt

2 tablespoons Chinese or Thai oyster sauce

1 egg, lightly beaten

FOR THE SOUP

1.75 l low-sodium vegetable or chicken stock

2-cm piece fresh ginger, cut into matchsticks

1 clove garlic, finely sliced

30 g sliced shiitake mushroom caps

12 small (10-cm) wonton wrappers (square or round), stacked and sliced into 5-mm-wide strips

MAKE THE MEATBALLS In a bowl, combine the pork, shrimp, bread crumbs, minced garlic, minced ginger, spring onions, coriander, jalapeño, salt, oyster sauce and beaten egg. Gently mix just to combine. (Be careful not to overdo it. Overdoing makes meatballs tough. A tough meatball just doesn't sound good.) Refrigerate while you make the soup.

MAKE THE SOUP In a medium (3-litre) saucepan, combine the stock, matchstick ginger and sliced garlic and bring to a simmer over high heat. Cover and simmer over very low heat for 15 minutes to let the flavours meld.

Using slightly wet hands, form the prawn–pork mixture into 4 equal meatballs. Gently lower the meatballs into the stock, then add the mushrooms. Bring to a simmer and cook until the meatballs are cooked through, about 12 minutes. During the last 3 minutes of cooking, add the wonton wrapper noodles and cook until opaque and tender.

Divide the meatballs, noodles and broth among four bowls and garnish with coriander, jalapeños and spring onions.

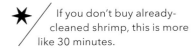 If you don't buy already-cleaned shrimp, this is more like 30 minutes.

CREAMY TOMATO SOUP
with Peppery Parmesan Crisps

Surely you know about my love affair with soup. And baby Luna has given me another love affair. No, not herself. I mean, I *do* love her and her epically chubby face (I've never seen a face before with four corners), but because of her I now have a love affair with all things EASYLICIOUS. Easylicious is easy *and* delicious and ughhhhhh I have the worst mum jokes please help me.

Anyway, this tomato soup is so simple, so creamy, and so easylicious that it will blow your mind. I took one bite of it and was like: Crap. It's perfect. I love it. But it's so *simple*. Does it need bacon?? Ham?? Cheese bombs?? But no. It doesn't. Like all the pretty-boy singers these days say: Sometimes simple is beautiful. Sometimes a soup looks better without bacon makeup. Sometimes soup doesn't even have to try.

Or you can try a *little* and impress everyone with a little crispy, Parmy frico chip on top. If you know how to shred cheese, you can Parmy frico.

SERVES 4
ACTIVE TIME / 5 MIN
TOTAL TIME / 35 MIN

3 tablespoons olive oil

1 medium onion, cut into 1-cm dice

4 cloves garlic, chopped

2 (400-g) cans whole peeled tomatoes in juice, roughly chopped (see Note)

250 ml low-sodium chicken or vegetable stock

½ teaspoon sugar, plus more to taste

Kosher salt and freshly ground black pepper

60 ml double, cream or more to taste

Parmesan Crisps (recipe follows), for serving

In a large saucepan, heat the oil over medium heat. Add the onion and cook, stirring, until translucent and golden, about 10 minutes. Add the garlic and cook 1 additional minute.

Add the tomatoes, their juice, the stock, sugar, 1 teaspoon salt, and ½ teaspoon pepper. Bring to a boil, reduce the heat to medium-low or low, and simmer gently until the liquid reduces slightly, about 15 minutes.

Let the soup cool for a few minutes, then pour it into a blender or food processor and blend on high speed (make sure to leave a little vent so steam can escape from the blender) until smooth, 1 to 2 minutes. Add the cream and blend a few seconds more. Season to taste with more salt, pepper and/or sugar.

Divide among bowls and serve with the Parmesan crisps.

Note
Use kitchen shears to cut the 'maters right in the can.

Parmesan Crisps

60 g finely grated Parmigiano-Reggiano cheese
Freshly ground black pepper

Preheat the oven to 375°F/190°C. Line a large baking sheet with parchment paper or a silicone baking mat.

Measure out a heaping tablespoon of cheese at a time and pile it on the baking sheet, spreading it out a little until it's about 3 inches in diameter – it doesn't have to be a perfect round! Grind fresh pepper on to each pile and bake until lightly golden and crisped, 5 to 6 minutes. Remove from the oven and transfer the whole sheet of crisps to the counter to cool (they will continue to crisp as they cool).

MAKES 8 CRISPS
ACTIVE TIME / 5 MIN
TOTAL TIME / 10 MIN
(unless you want to count the oven heating time but c'mon)

FRENCH ONION SOUP

I LOVE ONIONS. Sometimes I will dice raw, red onion and munch on it, which, by the way, means your liver isn't functioning properly and is craving the sulphur in an onion. So basically, eat one onion for every four shots of tequila.

I am absolutely obsessed with French onion soup. My favourite? At Balthazar in Soho, NYC. The bubbling cheese flows over the sides of the crock and the floating bread gently peeks out with its sexy golden edges ohhhhhhhhhhhh my God it's as beefy and rich as Mario Lopez.

And yet – mine is better. My personal favourite part about FOS is the half-inch layer of cheese you must break through to even attain soup. Mine has that half inch of cheese at the top AND cheese at the bottom. There is a cheese basement AND a cheese attic. And the soy sauce and red wine that bind all that beefy richness together? That's special as sh*t.

And did I mention the toasty, flaky, buttery croissant croutons? My only peeve with French onion soup is that I can't spoon-cut the baguette and must plow the entire piece into my mouth – which is fine, but then I'm out of bread for the rest of my soup. NOT OK. Now each bite is one part soup, one part oozy cheese, and one part crispy, melt-in-your-mouth croissant goodness. Every. Single. Bite.

SERVES 6
ACTIVE TIME / 15 MIN
TOTAL TIME / 1 HR 45 MIN

3 tablespoons olive oil

7 tablespoons butter

1.35 kg thinly sliced onions

5 thyme sprigs, tied into a bundle with kitchen twine

8 cloves garlic, thinly sliced

2 tablespoons plain flour

300 ml dry red wine

1.5 l beef stock

1½ tablespoons soy sauce (see Note)

Kosher salt

4 large croissants, cut into 3.5-cm cubes

340 g Gruyère or Swiss cheese, grated

In a really big (at least 7.5 liters) heavy-bottomed pot, heat the oil and 7 tablespoons of the butter over high heat. Add the onions and the thyme bundle and cook, stirring often, until the onions begin to shrink but are still light in colour, about 15 minutes. Reduce the heat to medium-low, add the garlic and cook, stirring often, until the onions are golden and meltingly tender, another 20 minutes, but really watch the colour more than the clock. If some of the onions are getting brown before the others are turning golden, stir more. You want all the onions to be beautifully, evenly golden brown.

Add the flour and cook, stirring, until it coats all the onions and makes them look kinda dull, about 3 minutes. Add the wine, increase the heat to medium, bring to a boil, and cook until the onions are purple and the wine has evaporated, about 5 minutes. Discard the thyme bundle. Add the stock, soy sauce and 1 teaspoon salt. Bring to a boil over high heat, reduce the heat again and cook at a gentle simmer until the soup has thickened and the onions are no longer purple, about 45 minutes. Season to taste with salt.

Preheat the oven to 350°F/175°C. Arrange the croissant pieces on a large baking sheet and bake until golden, about 9 minutes. Remove from the oven and heat the grill.

Arrange six 300-ml ovenproof soup crocks on a rimmed baking sheet. Mound half the Gruyère on the bottom of each crock. Ladle soup over the cheese, almost to the top. Top each soup with a few croissant croutons, then mound the rest of the Gruyère on top, mostly covering the croutons. Grill until the cheese is bubbling and slightly browned and the croutons are nice and toasty on the edges, 3 to 4 minutes (this time can depend on your grill, so check early and often!).

Note / *SOY SAUCE IS KING!*

It adds a super umami POW here, the kind you usually need to cook beef stock for 8 hours to get. If you can, get the good stuff; anything that tastes like more than just brown salt water (we use Kikkoman for our general soy sauce).

PARMESAN MINESTRONE
with Chilli Mayo Toasts

Few things on a menu are more trustworthy than minestrone. The worst thing that can happen is it comes out a little watery, but nothing horrid enough that you can't fix with a little salt. But the best that can happen? A rich, deeply flavourful soup bound together with Parmesan cheese. This version is like the soup you get in the can that you always love, only a little fresher (though, yes, hello, it's me, Chrissy, and I use three cans in the recipe; four, if you use stock from a can, too). Then, because sometimes more is more, I smeared Mom's hot chilli oil mixed with mayo all over some toasts and grilled them to use as little soup scoopers. Or if you hate soup, just eat the toasts and pass that bowl over here, thank you very much.

SERVES 8
ACTIVE TIME / 20 MIN
TOTAL TIME / 1 HR

3 tablespoons olive oil

1 large onion, cut into 1-cm dice

6 cloves garlic, minced

2 medium carrots, cut into 1-cm dice

2 celery stalks, cut into 1-cm dice

1.75 l vegetable or chicken stock

2 (400 g) cans diced tomatoes in juice

1 (400 g) can cannellini beans, drained and rinsed

1 (400 g) can green beans*, undrained

1 teaspoon dried basil

1 teaspoon dried oregano

Kosher salt and freshly ground black pepper

¼ teaspoon chilli flakes

50 g short pasta (we like wheels!)

80 g finely grated Parmigiano-Reggiano cheese, plus more for garnish

Chilli Mayo Toasts (recipe follows)

In a large soup pot, heat the oil over medium heat. Add the onion and cook until tender and translucent, about 8 minutes. Add the garlic and cook 1 additional minute. Add the carrots and celery and cook until slightly softened, about 4 minutes.

Add the stock, diced tomatoes, cannellini beans, green beans (with the liquid from the can), basil, oregano, 2½ teaspoons salt, ½ teaspoon black pepper and chilli flakes. Increase the heat to high, bring to a boil, then reduce to a simmer and cook until the liquid thickens slightly, about 20 minutes.

Add the pasta and cook until tender, another 10 minutes or so. Stir in the Parm and season to taste with salt and black pepper. Garnish with more Parm. Serve with the chilli mayo toasts.

If the soup cools completely, it'll thicken a lot because of the starch in the pasta. If it's too thick for you, add a little water or stock when you reheat it.

★ / Or use 100 g fresh green beans cut into 3-cm lengths plus 200 g water.

Chilli Mayo Toasts

MAKES 16 TOASTS
ACTIVE TIME / 5 MIN
TOTAL TIME / 8 MIN

16 thin slices baguette

Chilli Oil (page 160)

Mayonnaise

Kosher salt and freshly ground black pepper

Preheat the grill to low (or if you just have one grill setting, position the oven rack so it's not right under the element).

Brush one side of the toasts with a bit of chilli oil (the bread will drink in the oil), then spread each toast with a light layer of mayo and season with salt and pepper to taste. Grill on a baking sheet until golden and toasty, watching so the bread doesn't burn, 1 to 3 minutes depending on the grill.

Bacony
CLAM
CHOWDER

The word 'chowder' just screams comfort to me. It makes me think of a snowy little town with hilly streets and a main street lined with pubs and antique shops. A town where I *belong* in some sort of alternate life. I craaaaave steaming bowls of chowder and the accompanying plastic bag of crackers.

     If you were to make this soup using fresh clams, you'd need to find EIGHT POUNDS WORTH. So, as much as I love the idea of hauling Luna's body weight in seafood home from the store, I think I may be saying good-bye to the process of cleaning, steaming, cooling and stripping those little shell houses of their precious meat until further notice. And really, canned clams don't suck – just make sure to save the juice they're swimming in because it gives this creamy broth its special oceany flavour. They are hard to find in the UK unless you shop online but worth the effort!

SERVES 6
ACTIVE TIME / 20 MIN
TOTAL TIME / 1 HR

5 thick slices bacon, cut into ¼-inch pieces

3 tablespoons butter

1 small onion, finely chopped

2 celery stalks, diced

1 large carrot, diced

2 cloves garlic, thinly sliced

5 tablespoons plain flour

500 ml vegetable stock

2 (300 g) cans clams in juice, liquid drained and reserved

450 g (2 medium) King Edward potatoes, peeled and cut into 1.5-cm chunks

1 bay leaf

Kosher salt

¼ teaspoon cayenne pepper, or to taste

300 ml double or single cream

Freshly ground black pepper

Chopped fresh parsley, for garnish

Cholula or Crystal hot sauce

In a large pot, cook the bacon over medium heat until browned, 6 to 8 minutes. Drain all but 2 tablespoons of the bacon fat, add the butter, then add the onion, celery and carrot and cook, stirring, until softened, about 5 minutes. Add the garlic and cook 1 additional minute.

Add the flour and stir until it disappears into the vegetables, about 1 minute. Add the vegetable stock and clam juice (they should total 1 litre*), the potatoes, bay leaf, 1½ teaspoons salt and the cayenne. Bring to a simmer, reduce the heat, and keep at a simmer, stirring occasionally, for 10 minutes. Add the cream and simmer until the potatoes are tender, about another 15 minutes.

Add the clams and cook for about 2 minutes to just warm through. Season to taste with salt and pepper. Ladle into bowls and garnish with parsley. Serve with hot sawwwwce.

★ You need a total of 1 litre liquid (vegetable stock plus clam juice), so add more stock or water if there's not enough clam juice.

CARROT COCONUT SOUP

SERVES 4
ACTIVE TIME / 10 MIN
TOTAL TIME / 1 HR 10 MIN

If you lined this soup up next to a bowl of Luna's carrot baby food . . . you *might* have to look twice to tell the difference. But THAT IS WHERE THE SIMILARITIES END. I lace my carrot coconut soup with both Thai sweet chilli sauce and my hot chilli oil for a yin-yangy bowl of deliciousness. (Of course, you can adjust the amount of one over the other if you tend toward spicier or sweeter.) The key is to get the soup really smooth with a blender, immersion blender, or food processor. Bright, beautiful, clean, with a hint of spice – just like you, boo.

4 tablespoons butter

1 small onion, chopped

Kosher salt

¼ teaspoon freshly ground black pepper

450 g carrots, chopped

500 ml low-sodium chicken or vegetable stock

1 (400 ml) can full-fat coconut milk, shaken

1 stalk fresh lemongrass, trimmed (see Tip, page 99)

1 teaspoon finely grated fresh ginger

2 tablespoons Thai sweet chilli sauce

Chilli Oil (page 160) and/or Crispy Shallots (page 130), for serving

Coriander, for garnish

In a medium-large pot, heat the butter over medium heat. Once foamy and sliiiiiiiiiightly browned, add the onion, 1 teaspoon salt and the pepper and cook, stirring, until the onion just begins to soften, about 2 minutes. Add the carrots and cook, stirring, until softened and the onion has turned deep golden, 18 to 20 minutes (some bits of the onion will turn a little darker than others – it's cool).

Add the chicken stock, coconut milk, lemongrass and ginger. Bring to a boil, reduce the heat to a very low simmer, cover (leave the lid open a crack), walk away for 40 minutes, and totally forget about the soup because your baby hit you on purpose for the first time.

Stir in the sweet chilli sauce, remove from the heat, and let cool slightly. Remove and discard the lemongrass. Blend the soup in the pot with a stick blender (or in a stand blender) until smooth. (If using a stand blender, hold the lid on tight and make sure to leave a little vent so steam can escape from the blender; protect your hand with an oven mitt or towel.) Season to taste with salt.

Divide among bowls and top with chilli oil and/or crispy shallots. Garnish with coriander.

SALADS

Cool Ranch
TACO SALAD

Have I ever told you about the time Taco Bell invited me to their headquarters for a Taco Bell Friendsgiving? I'd never seen anything like it. They had the head chef, who develops all their menu items (yes, he is a real chef, assholes), give all the Thanksgiving trimmings a Taco Bell spin. I laughed at how gross this sounded but . . . oh, how I was wrong. After the epic dinner, they showed us all the secret items they were testing and I was lucky enough to try, and fall in love with, the Doritos Locos Taco.

I had dreams of finding out what the hell is in the seasoning for Cool Ranch Doritos here in the US, but even if I did find it, I can't do that to you. Forcing you to make Cool Ranch dust for this downhome, family-staple taco salad would be very Book 1. Book 2, post-Luna Chrissy says to buy a bag and crush them up. Who knows what laziness Book 3 Chrissy will come up with, at this baby-making rate.

SERVES 6 AS A MAIN COURSE OR 8 TO 10 AS AN APPETIZER
ACTIVE TIME / 20 MIN
TOTAL TIME / 50 MIN

FOR THE DRESSING
170 ml vegetable oil

60 ml ketchup

60 ml distilled white vinegar

1 tablespoon sugar

½ teaspoon kosher salt

½ teaspoon cayenne pepper

FOR THE BEEF MIXTURE
2 large ears corn, husked, or 200 g frozen sweetcorn kernels, thawed and patted dry

1 tablespoon rapeseed oil

1 pound minced beef

1 tablespoon paprika*

2 teaspoons ground cumin*

2 teaspoons garlic powder*

2 teaspoons dried oregano*

1 teaspoon cayenne pepper*

1½ teaspoons kosher salt*

1 teaspoon freshly ground black pepper*

1 (400 g) can black beans, drained and rinsed

30 g chopped fresh coriander

FOR THE SALAD
1 large head iceberg lettuce, shredded

2 beef tomatoes, cut into chunks

1 large avocado, cut into chunks

50 g sliced black olives (optional)

120 g Cool Doritos (or other tortilla chips if that's what you've got)

40 g chopped red onion

125 ml sour cream

MAKE THE DRESSING In a screw-top jar, shake to mix the oil, ketchup, vinegar, sugar, salt and cayenne.

MAKE THE BEEF MIXTURE Heat a large dry frying pan over high heat until really hot. Put the whole ears of corn in the pan and DFWI (Don't F*ck With It!!) until the underside is charred, about 3 minutes. Keep cooking, turning two more times, until the corn is charred in spots all over, 8 to 9 minutes. Remove to a plate. (If using thawed frozen kernels, char them in the dry pan in a single layer, only stirring once or twice, until slightly blackened, about 6 minutes.)

Let the pan cool a bit. Add the oil and heat over medium-high heat until shimmering-hot. Add the meat, breaking it up, until cooked through, 5 to 6 minutes.

Drain most of the liquid from the pan but leave enough to keep the meat juicy. In a small bowl, combine the paprika, cumin, garlic powder, oregano, cayenne, salt and black pepper. Add the spice mixture to the meat along with the black beans and 125 ml water. Cook, stirring gently, 5 minutes. Remove from the heat, let cool slightly, and stir in the coriander.

MAKE THE SALAD Arrange the lettuce in a big salad bowl and top with the beef-bean mixture. Cut the corn from the cobs and add it to the salad with the tomatoes, avocado and olives (if using). Pour the dressing over the salad and crumble the chips all over the top. Sprinkle with the onion and top with the sour cream.

Or a packet of taco seasoning.

Roasted
CARROT & AVOCADO SALAD
with Lime Dressing

Once upon a time, avocados had a purpose in life beyond smashing themselves on top of toast and waiting for a close-up. They hung out in salads like this one, mingling with all the other ingredients and doing their part for salad glory. That time has returned, avocados. So play nicely with the roasted carrots, limey dressing, and crunchy seeds and everyone will get along just fine.

SERVES 4
ACTIVE TIME / 10 MIN
TOTAL TIME / 30 MIN

FOR THE CARROTS

2 tablespoons olive oil

4 cloves garlic, finely chopped

1 teaspoon kosher salt

¼ teaspoon freshly ground black pepper

¼ teaspoon cayenne pepper

450 g thin carrots, (halved lengthwise if thicker than 2 cm)

FOR THE DRESSING

3 tablespoons olive oil

1 teaspoon grated lime zest

1 tablespoon fresh lime juice

½ teaspoon kosher salt

¼ teaspoon freshly ground black pepper

⅛ teaspoon cayenne pepper

FOR THE SALAD

2 little gem lettuces

1 firm-ripe avocado, sliced (see Tip, page 65)

3 tablespoons salted lightly toasted sunflower seeds (store-bought or see Tip)

Kosher salt and freshly ground black pepper

ROAST THE CARROTS Preheat the oven to 400°F/200°C. In a large bowl, whisk the oil, garlic, salt, pepper and cayenne. Add the carrots and toss to coat. Dump them on to a large rimmed baking sheet, spread them into one layer, and roast until the carrots are caramelized and roasted but not mushy, 20 to 25 minutes. Let them cool slightly.

MAKE THE DRESSING In a screw-top jar, combine the olive oil, lime zest, lime juice, salt, black pepper and cayenne and shake until creamy and emulsified.

ASSEMBLE THE SALAD Arrange the lettuce on a serving platter. Top with the roasted carrots, then scatter the avocado slices on top. Drizzle with the dressing to taste, sprinkle on the sunflower seeds and season to taste with salt and pepper.

Tip / HOW TO TOAST THOSE SEEDS

In a small ungreased frying pan, toast the sunflower seeds over medium-low heat until fragrant, 4 to 5 minutes. Transfer to a plate to cool and season lightly with salt.

GOAT CHEESE NIÇOISE
with Crispy Olive Oil Toasts

John cannot help but order this if his eyes catch it on a menu. A Niçoise is more than a salad . . . it's like a cooking lesson (but an easy one, don't sweat it). You start with one pot of cold water and end up with perfect potatoes, green beans and hard-boiled eggs one after the other. It's all about timing here, so don't get distracted by how pretty the green beans are when you shock 'em under cold water, or how those yolks look like the sunrise, or how comfortable your bathrobe is and why would you wear anything else while cooking. (P.S. You will also learn how to grill fresh tuna, something almost as laughably easy as opening and draining a can.)

SERVES 4 AS A MAIN
COURSE OR 6 AS A FIRST
COURSE
ACTIVE TIME / 30 MIN
TOTAL TIME / 45 MIN

FOR THE TOASTS

12 thin slices baguette

Olive oil, for brushing

Kosher salt and freshly ground black pepper

FOR THE DRESSING

60 ml olive oil

2 tablespoons fresh lemon juice

2 teaspoons fish sauce

1 teaspoon Dijon mustard

½ teaspoon freshly ground black pepper

FOR THE SALAD

Kosher salt

450 g potatoes (4 small or 2 medium), scrubbed

225 g green beans, trimmed

4 eggs

450-g tuna steak

Freshly ground black pepper

1 head round lettuce or 2 little gem lettuces, chopped

2 medium tomatoes, cut into wedges

110 g goat cheese, pinched with your fingers into chunks

A handful of sliced Kalamata olives (optional)

MAKE THE TOASTS Preheat the oven to 350°F/170°C. Arrange the baguette on a baking sheet. Brush one side lightly with olive oil and season with salt and pepper. Bake until toasty and crisp, 8 to 10 minutes.

MAKE THE DRESSING In a screw-top jar, combine the oil, lemon juice, fish sauce, mustard and pepper and shake until creamy.

MAKE THE SALAD In a large pot, cover the potatoes with heavily salted cold water. Bring to a boil, then reduce to a simmer and cook the potatoes until they are easily pierced with a fork but not mushy (you're going to slice these and eat them in the salad, not mash them), 20 to 25 minutes. Remove the potatoes with a slotted spoon (don't drain the water; you're reusing it!) and cool on a plate. When they're cool enough to handle, cut them into chunks or slices (you do you).

Set up a large bowl filled with really icy water. Bring the potato-cooking water back to a boil. Drop the green beans into the pot and cook just until they turn bright green and soften slightly, about 2 minutes. Pull them out with a slotted spoon or a strainer and drop them into the ice water bath. (Keep the water boiling.)

Gently lower the eggs into the boiling water and cook for 6 minutes for soft, slightly undercooked yolks and 8 minutes for more hard-boiled eggs.

While the eggs are cooking, remove the green beans from the ice water bath (don't drain the ice water, either), drain on paper towels, and cut into 2-inch lengths.

Remove the eggs with a slotted spoon and drop them into the ice water to cool for about 5 minutes (add a few more ice cubes to the water if you need to chill it down). Remove, peel and quarter the eggs.

Preheat a frying pan or griddle pan over medium-high heat. Pat the tuna dry with paper towels and season well with salt and pepper. Griddle for 2 to 3 minutes per side, watching the sides of the steak until the uncooked centre of the fish is equal in height to the cooked layer on each side. Remove to a plate, let cool and slice.

Arrange the lettuce in a salad bowl and top with the tomatoes, green beans, potatoes, eggs, goat cheese and olives (if using). Top with slices of tuna and dress with some of the dressing. Serve with the rest of the dressing and the toasts on the side (or crumble the toasts on top like croutons).

Asian Pear &
AVOCADO SALAD

One thing that's gotten me through life is that I am not allergic to peanut oil, because if I was, my mom, Pepper Thai, would have traded me in for a better, hardier model. Thankfully I can enjoy this toasty nutty dressing as is, but if you need to fink out with rapeseed oil (or can't find peanut), know that I would NOT trade you in for anyone else.

The dressing is great with pears, especially Asian pears. Sometimes Asian pears are called apple or Nashi pears because they're super crunchy and probably also because you need to appeal to the racist customers who won't eat something called 'Asian'. You'll find them in the store, often individually dressed in their own little stretchy foam jackets because they are extra fancy and special (and they do cost a little more than your average pear).

SERVES 6 TO 8
ACTIVE TIME / 15 MIN
TOTAL TIME / 15 MIN

250 g mixed greens of your choice

30 g fresh regular or Thai basil leaves, torn

1 crisp Asian pear or very firm regular pear, cored and thinly sliced

½ red onion, thinly sliced

Sesame Ginger Dressing (recipe follows)

1 firm-ripe avocado, peeled (see Tip) and sliced

50 g sliced almonds, lightly toasted

In a large salad bowl, toss together the greens, basil, pear and onion. Gently toss in the dressing to taste, the avocado, and most of the almonds. Garnish with the remaining almonds.

Tip / KEEP IT GREEN

To keep the halved avo from browning before you slice it, press plastic wrap directly on to the avo's surface. (Oxygen causes the darkening so, yes, technically you're suffocating the avocado. Sorry, let's not talk about it.)

Sesame Ginger / Dressing /

85 ml mayonnaise

85 ml peanut oil

2 tablespoons rice vinegar

2 tablespoons sesame oil

1 tablespoon fresh lime juice

2 teaspoons sugar

1 teaspoon Sriracha, or more to taste

1 teaspoon kosher salt

1-cm piece fresh ginger, peeled

1 clove garlic, peeled

In a blender, combine the mayo, peanut oil, vinegar, sesame oil, lime juice, sugar, Sriracha, salt, ginger and garlic and blend until smooth. (Or you can finely mince the ginger and garlic and shake all the ingredients in a jar until smooth and creamy.) Refrigerate until ready to use.

MAKES 250 ML
ACTIVE TIME / 5 MIN
TOTAL TIME / 5 MIN

Roasted BUTTERNUT SQUASH & POMEGRANATE SALAD with Garlicky Honey-Dijon Dressing

Salads can be so basic. Why bother? Wellllllllll because roasted squash and little pom jewels that burst in your mouth and creamy goat cheese and a dressing you'll want to put on all your other green leafy things are *magic*.

SERVES 4 TO 6
ACTIVE TIME / 20 MIN
TOTAL TIME / 1 HR

FOR THE SQUASH

3 tablespoons olive oil

675 g 1-cm cubes peeled butternut squash

1½ teaspoons kosher salt

½ teaspoon freshly ground black pepper

¼ to ½ teaspoon cayenne pepper, to taste

FOR THE DRESSING

2 tablespoons white wine vinegar or apple cider vinegar

1 tablespoon Dijon mustard

1 tablespoon honey

1 clove garlic, grated or smashed into a paste

¼ teaspoon kosher salt

¼ teaspoon freshly ground black pepper

3 tablespoons olive oil

FOR THE SALAD

100 g baby rocket

85 g pomegranate seeds* (see Tip)

15 g pumpkin seeds, lightly toasted

½ small red onion, thinly sliced

100 g crumbled goat cheese

Freshly ground black pepper

ROAST THE SQUASH Preheat the oven to 400°F/200°C. Line a rimmed baking sheet with foil and pour 2 tablespoons of the oil on the lined sheet. Place the oiled sheet in the oven (yep, nothing on it) and heat until very hot but not smoking, about 8 minutes.

In a large bowl, toss the squash with the remaining 1 tablespoon oil, the salt, pepper and cayenne until coated. Using an oven mitt, remove the hot baking sheet from the oven and quickly pour the squash on to the sheet (you should hear some sizzling); take a few extra seconds to make sure the flat sides of the squash are hitting that hot oiled pan. Roast until the undersides are golden, about 15 minutes. Remove the squash from the oven, shake the pan (or flip the squash with tongs if you're down with OCD, yeah you know me), return to the oven, and roast until the new underside is golden brown, 10 to 15 minutes. Let cool to room temp or just warm (so it doesn't murder the greens when you drop them on).

MAKE THE DRESSING In a screw-top jar, shake the vinegar, mustard, honey, garlic, salt, pepper and oil until it's creamy. (If it separates, just shake it again.)

MAKE THE SALAD Arrange the rocket on a platter. Top with the roasted squash, pomegranate seeds and pumpkin seeds. Scatter the onion and goat cheese on top. Drizzle with the dressing to taste and sprinkle with pepper.

 Or finely diced green apple if you can't find pom seeds.

Tip / *HOW TO SEED A POMEGRANATE WITHOUT STAINING YOUR LIFE RED*

Fill a large bowl with cold water. Use a sharp knife to cut about halfway through the pomegranate, then split the pomegranate apart underwater. Pull the seeds off the white stuff (it's called pith); the seeds will sink to the bottom and most of the white stuff will float to the top. Drain the water and floaty white bits from the bowl, then pick out any remaining white stuff from the seeds.

Tangy Herb-Sesame
SLAW

Cabbage salad doesn't *have* to be a mayo-soaked mess. In fact it can be a clean, crunchy thing you just pull out of the fridge and snack on without feeling like you drank a salad cream chaser. (No shade.) This is a really good oil-and-vinegar slaw that uses sh*t you definitely already have in the pantry. This, underneath sweet chicken drummies (or really ANYTHING), is like a crunchy blanket of dessert cabbage. That . . . didn't sound as great as I wanted it to, but just trust me. Make it, eat it, and report back to me.

SERVES 6 TO 8
ACTIVE TIME / 20 MIN
TOTAL TIME / 20 MIN

FOR THE DRESSING

85 ml vegetable oil

85 ml unseasoned rice vinegar

2 tablespoons soy sauce

1 tablespoon honey

1 tablespoon Dijon mustard

1 tablespoon toasted sesame oil

3 cloves garlic, finely minced

FOR THE SALAD

¼ head shredded red cabbage

½ small head shredded Chinese cabbage

4 spring onions, thinly sliced

1 large carrot, shredded

30 g chopped fresh coriander

15 g chopped fresh mint

15 g chopped fresh basil

100 g chopped roasted peanuts

30 g toasted sesame seeds

MAKE THE DRESSING In a screw-top jar, combine the vegetable oil, vinegar, soy sauce, honey, mustard, sesame oil and garlic and shake until incorporated.

ASSEMBLE THE SALAD In a large bowl, toss the cabbages, spring onions, carrot, coriander, mint, basil, peanuts and sesame seeds together with the dressing to taste, holding back some of the peanuts and sesame seeds for garnish. Garnish with the reserved peanuts and sesame seeds.

SANDWI

CHES

CHICKEN TERIYAKI BURGERS
with Toasted Coco Buns

I'm not gonna spend too much time here selling you on teriyaki burgers. They're freaking fantastic. Juicy, sweet little patty babies oozing with flavor and drips of sweet pineapple. But the real story are the coconut buns. How on earth did it take until this year to cross my mind to slather bread with butter and a sprinkling of coconut? It might be the easiest thing I've ever done that has ever completely taken a recipe to the next level. Do them at the very last minute while people are watching so you can show off your toasty golden buns like the hero you are.

SERVES 4
ACTIVE TIME / 30 MIN
TOTAL TIME / 1 HR 10 MIN
(includes chilling)

FOR THE BURGERS

15 g fresh bread crumbs (see page 178)

450 g ground chicken

15 g chopped fresh coriander

3 spring onions, thinly sliced

2 tablespoons minced fresh ginger

3 cloves garlic, minced

1 egg

3 tablespoons soy sauce

1½ tablespoons dark brown sugar

1 tablespoon sesame oil

1 tablespoon chilli paste, such as sambal oelek

1 teaspoon kosher salt

4 round slices (5-mm thick) red onion

Rapeseed oil, for brushing

4 rings (1-cm thick) fresh pineapple (or 4 canned rings, drained and patted dry)

FOR ASSEMBLY

125 ml mayonnaise

2 teaspoons Sriracha

4 hamburger buns

5½ tablespoons butter, at room temperature

35 g unsweetened finely shredded coconut

8 small round lettuce leaves

MAKE THE BURGERS In a large bowl, gently combine the bread crumbs, chicken, coriander, spring onions, ginger and garlic. In a small bowl, whisk together the egg, soy sauce, brown sugar, sesame oil, chilli paste and salt. Fold into the burger mix. Using your hands, form the mixture into four 2.5-cm-thick burgers and chill on a plate for at least 30 minutes.

Preheat a griddle pan over medium-high heat. Brush the onion rounds with some oil.

Grill the burgers, onion rings and pineapple until the burgers form grill marks and are cooked about halfway through, 4 minutes. Flip the burgers, pineapple rings and onions (it's OK if the onions fall apart) and grill until the burgers are cooked through and the onions and pineapple rings are softened and charred, another 3 to 4 minutes.

While the burgers are cooking, preheat the grill. (Use a low setting, or position the rack to be a little farther away from the heat.)

ASSEMBLE THE BURGERS In a small bowl, combine the mayo and Sriracha. Split all the buns and put them on a baking sheet. Butter each bun half with about 2 teaspoons butter and sprinkle each with 1 tablespoon coconut. Grill until toasty and the butter bubbles, about 2 minutes (watch carefully). Spread some Sriracha mayo on the bottom half of each bun. Stack 2 pieces of lettuce and top with a pineapple ring, a burger and some of the onions. Top each sandwich with a toasted coco bun half.

Jalapeño Parmesan-Crusted CHEESE TOASTIES

Once upon a (brief) time, I was on a daytime television talk show with three really wonderful people. One of my favourite things I had . . . *got* . . . to do was a food truck takeover: the famed L.A. Grilled Cheese Truck. (GET THE TATER TOTS IF YOU SEE THIS BABY PULLED OVER!) My mouth was treated to a 'Grilled Chrissy' that I will never forget. In an American era where we stuff *anything* we can with cheese, it never crossed my mind to both stuff AND coat something in it. But this is how we live now, people.

SERVES 2
ACTIVE TIME / 10 MIN
TOTAL TIME / 15 MIN

- **3 tablespoons butter, at room temperature**
- **4 slices soft sourdough bread**
- **1 small jalapeño, sliced into thin rings**
- **80 g finely grated Parmigiano-Reggiano cheese**
- **90 g shredded extra-sharp cheddar cheese**

Spread one side of each slice of bread with about 2 teaspoons softened butter. Arrange 4 or 5 jalapeño rings over the butter on each slice, pressing down to make them stick. Place the Parm in a shallow dish and press the buttered, jalapeño side of each slice of bread into the Parm. Scatter half of the cheddar on the unbuttered side of each of 2 slices, then close the sandwiches (all the Parmed sides on the outside).

Heat a nonstick frying pan over medium-low heat. Add the sandwiches and cook, covered, until the underside is golden but not burnt, 2 to 3 minutes. Flip and cook, covered, until the underside is golden but not burnt and the edges are crisp, 2 to 3 minutes.

Fried Pork
BÁNH MÌ SANDWICHES
with Quick Pickles

After making these sandwiches (that's what *bánh mì* actually means in Vietnamese) once, you are going to make them again. And again. Especially after realizing that the thin-sliced pork marinates in the time it takes you to make the sweet-and-sour pickled vegetables, which are ready in about as much as time it takes to run out and buy some fresh bread. (The bread is pretty important here: Go for soft, baguette-ish rolls.) You fry that pork for just a couple minutes until it caramelizes, then layer it on the toasted bread with the pickles and squiggles of mayo and Sriracha. Crunchy, juicy, porky, sweet, tart, salty, colourful – it's all there on a roll.

SERVES 4
ACTIVE TIME / 45 MIN
TOTAL TIME / 1 HR 45 MIN

FOR THE PICKLES

1 large carrot, shredded

2 small cucumbers, sliced into ribbons with a vegetable peeler

½ small onion, sliced into thin rings

125 ml unseasoned rice vinegar

140 g granulated sugar

1 teaspoon kosher salt

5 black peppercorns

1 fresh chilli, halved lengthwise

FOR THE PORK

550 g pork tenderloin

100 g light brown sugar

3 tablespoons soy sauce

3 tablespoons rapeseed oil

Grated zest of 1 lime

2 tablespoons fresh lime juice

1 tablespoon fish sauce

1 shallot, thinly sliced

2 cloves garlic, very thinly sliced

1 tablespoon Sriracha

¼ teaspoon ground white pepper

FOR THE SANDWICHES

4 half baguettes, split and toasted

Mayonnaise

Sriracha

120 g fresh coriander leaves

MAKE THE PICKLES In a heatproof medium bowl, combine the carrot, cucumbers and onion. In a small saucepan, bring the vinegar, granulated sugar, salt, peppercorns and chilli to a boil. Reduce the heat and simmer for 3 minutes, then remove from the heat and let cool for 5 minutes. Pour over the vegetables and toss to coat. Cover and refrigerate for at least 1 hour. Pickles will keep, chilled in the brine, for 1 week.

MAKE THE PORK Using a very sharp knife, cut the pork into 5-mm-thick medallions. In a medium bowl, combine the brown sugar, soy sauce, oil, lime zest, lime juice, fish sauce, shallot, garlic, Sriracha and white pepper. Add the pork and toss to coat. Cover and refrigerate for at least 1 hour and up to 4 hours. Drain the pork.

Heat a heavy frying pan or griddle pan over medium-high heat until super hot. Add the pork, spreading it out as best you can, and sear until dark and caramelized, 2 to 3 minutes (try not to move the meat around a lot!), then flip it to finish cooking, another 2 to 3 minutes.

ASSEMBLE THE SANDWICHES Spread a generous amount of mayo on both sides of each baguette and squiggle with some Sriracha. Pile about a quarter of the pickles (shake 'em dry!) on the bottom half of each baguette. Top each sandwich with one-quarter of the grilled pork and a quarter of the coriander leaves. Close the sandwiches and cut in half.

Sweet & Spicy
Peach & Brie
CHEESE TOASTIES

I threw fruit into this sandwich because I liked the idea of a cheese plate smashed between two buttery slices of bread. (Go for plums or nectarines if a peach isn't within reach.) And while I love me some Brie, I may love the Thai sweet chilli sauce even more. I use it up faster than A.1. sauce (similar to HP Sauce), which is . . . fast. I place bets with people and I take shots with it. Sometimes it is for no money. I just say, 'Wanna bet I can do seven shots of A.1. sauce?' And they're like, 'OK, how much?' And I'm like, 'Nothing, I just want A.1. sauce.' I like sweet chilli even more than that.

SERVES 4
ACTIVE TIME / 15 MIN
TOTAL TIME / 25 MIN

5½ tablespoons butter, at room temperature

8 slices soft, pillowy white bread

125 ml Thai sweet chilli sauce, plus more for dipping

½ red onion, thinly sliced

225 g cold Brie cheese, cut into 4 equal pieces (you can eat the rind if you want!)

1 juicy ripe peach, pitted and thinly sliced

Kosher salt

Spread one side of each slice of bread with about 2 teaspoons of the softened butter.

Arrange the bread, butter-side down, on a piece of parchment paper or a baking sheet. Spread 1 tablespoon of the Thai chilli sauce on the unbuttered sides.

Layer 4 slices of the bread with some onion slices, a piece of the Brie and a few peach slices. Season with salt. Set the other slices of bread, butter-side up, over the bottoms.

Heat a large frying pan or griddle over medium-high heat for 2 to 3 minutes.

Add 2 of the sandwiches to the pan and cook until the underside is golden and toasty and the cheese begins to melt, pressing down with a spatula or a sandwich press, 2 to 3 minutes. Flip the sandwiches and cook until the cheese melts and the underside is deep golden brown, another 2 to 3 minutes.

Wipe any burnt bits out of the pan with a paper towel and repeat with the remaining sandwiches.

Cheesy Knife-&-Fork MEATBALL SUBS

I think I've lived within a mile of a Subway sandwich shop my entire life, so basically I have consumed approximately 8.1 million meatballs, which makes me just 0.9 million meatballs away from being an expert meatball connoisseur. And now you've just learned I am one of the few complete psychopaths out there who actually gets the meatball sub at Subway.

My meatballs are like if Subway's meatballs were real meatballs made by a human. They're fluffy, moist, tender. The sauce (that needs to be jarred and sold immediately with a straw you could drink it with) oooooooozes into the toasty hot dog buns garlic bread.

These meatballs are the ONLY thing that got me through the horror that was November 8, 2016. I think I managed to keep them down for two hours.

SERVES 4
ACTIVE TIME / 45 MIN
TOTAL TIME / 1 HR 30 MIN

FOR THE SAUCE

- 6 tablespoons olive oil
- 1 jumbo onion, finely chopped
- 8 cloves garlic, minced
- 125 ml tomato paste
- 3 (400-g) cans whole peeled tomatoes in juice
- 2 teaspoons dried oregano
- 2 teaspoons dried basil
- 2 teaspoons kosher salt
- 2 teaspoons sugar

FOR THE MEATBALLS

- 50 g fresh bread crumbs (see page 178)
- 85 ml whole milk
- 1 egg, beaten
- 225 g ground beef
- 225 g ground pork
- 60 g finely grated Parmigiano-Reggiano cheese
- 1 tablespoon finely minced garlic
- 1½ teaspoons kosher salt
- ¼ teaspoon freshly ground black pepper
- 1 teaspoon dried oregano
- 1 teaspoon dried basil
- 3 tablespoons olive oil

FOR THE SUBS

- 4 plain old hot dog buns (nothing fancy)
- 4 tablespoons butter, at room temperature
- Garlic salt
- 8 round slices provolone cheese, halved (or Mozzarella)
- Chopped flat-leaf parsley, for garnish (optional)

CONTINUES

MAKE THE SAUCE In a wide soup pot, heat the oil over medium-high heat. Add the onion and cook, stirring, until golden, 8 to 9 minutes. Add the garlic and cook 1 additional minute. Add the tomato paste and cook, stirring, for 2 minutes. Add the tomatoes, their juice, the oregano, basil, salt and sugar. Bring to a boil, then reduce the heat and simmer until thickened, about 30 minutes. Blend the sauce in the pot with a stick blender (or in two batches in a stand blender) until smooth. Return the sauce to a simmer and cook for an additional 15 minutes. (You should have about 750 ml sauce.)

MEANWHILE, FORM THE MEATBALLS Place the bread crumbs in a large bowl. Add the milk, stir to moisten, and let the bread crumbs soak up the milk for 5 minutes. Stir in the egg. Add the beef, pork, Parm, garlic, salt, pepper, oregano and basil and gently mix everything together with your hands, being careful not to overmix the meat (that leads to tough balls). Moisten your hands and form the mixture into 12 meatballs, each slightly larger than a golf ball.

In a frying pan, heat the oil over medium heat. Add the meatballs and brown on all sides, turning so they don't get too crusty, 5 to 6 minutes total. When the sauce is ready, gently drop the meatballs into the sauce, cover, and simmer over low heat until the meatballs have cooked through, about 30 minutes.

MAKE THE SUBS Preheat the grill.

Split the rolls open, spread with the softened butter, and sprinkle them with as much garlic salt as you want (in my case, obvs, a lot). Place each roll on a heatproof plate or dish and grill until golden, 2 to 3 minutes. Arrange 3 meatballs, 4 provolone halves, and some sauce on top of each grilled bun and return to the grill until the cheese is melted and bubbling, another 2 minutes or so. Garnish with parsley, if you want.

Extra sauce can be stored in the fridge in an airtight container for up to 4 days, or frozen for up to 1 month.

PULLED BBQ CHICKEN SANDWICHES
with Pineapple Slaw

Barbecuing chicken is actually riskier than you think. Left in the hands of an amateur, the chicken can come out dry and blahhh. But what if you make pulled chicken by bathing the chicken in homemade barbecue sauce and letting it soak in all of that sweet and tangy deliciousness? What if you top it with a fresh slaw and surround it with the miracle of sandwich-making known as King's Hawaiian rolls? I have fixed your dry-ass barbecue.

    Also, this is make-in-the-pot-and-leave-it-there-until-ready-to-use food . . . which, in my book (and by that I also mean *this* book) is a check in the plus column. Not only that . . . but you make extra chicken and guess what? It goes on top of the chicken nachos somewhere else in this book (page 102). In the B.L.E. (Before Luna Era), these kinds of make-and-save recipes seemed kind of oh-yeah-great-idea, but in the A.L.E.? Pure cooking *gold*.

SERVES 6
ACTIVE TIME / 30 MIN
TOTAL TIME / 1 HR 40 MIN

FOR THE PULLED BBQ CHIC KEN

- **575 g boneless, skinless chicken thighs**
- **Kosher salt and freshly ground black pepper**
- **2 tablespoons rapeseed oil**
- **1 small onion, thinly sliced**
- **3 cloves garlic, minced**
- **2 tablespoons tomato paste**
- **125 ml ketchup**
- **85 ml tomato sauce**
- **60 ml apple cider vinegar**
- **2 tablespoons dark brown sugar**
- **1 tablespoon finely chopped canned chipotle in adobo sauce (leave the seeds in and even add more if you want it spicy) (available online if you can't find it in stores)**
- **1 teaspoon mustard powder**

FOR THE SLAW

- **225 g shredded green cabbage**
- **225 g shredded red cabbage**
- **1 small carrot, grated**
- **2 spring onions, thinly sliced**
- **15 g fresh or canned pineapple chunks (drained if canned), finely chopped**
- **185 ml mayonnaise**
- **2 tablespoons apple cider vinegar**
- **1½ teaspoons granulated sugar (optional)**
- **½ teaspoon kosher salt**
- **½ teaspoon freshly ground black pepper (available online)**

- **6 King's Hawaiian rolls (available online) or 6 soft burger buns (toasted if you want)**

CONTINUES

MAKE THE PULLED BBQ CHICKEN Season the chicken generously with salt and pepper. In a medium casserole dish, heat the oil over medium-high heat until shimmering-hot. Add the chicken in one layer (work in batches if you have to) and brown it until golden all over, 3 to 4 minutes per side. Transfer to a plate and set aside.

Add the onion to the pan and cook, stirring, until golden, 9 to 10 minutes. Add the garlic and cook 2 more minutes. Add the tomato paste and cook, stirring, for 2 minutes. Add the ketchup, tomato sauce, 60 ml water, vinegar, brown sugar, chipotles, mustard powder, ½ teaspoon salt, and ½ teaspoon pepper. Bring to a boil, reduce to a simmer, and cook uncovered until the sauce is thick, about 4 to 5 minutes.

Return the chicken and any juices to the pan, cover, and simmer until the chicken is very tender, about 1 hour. Add a few splashes of water if necessary to keep it from getting too dry. Remove from the heat and let cool. Shred the chicken with two forks right in the sauce (it will be pretty easy to shred). Keep covered in the casserole dish until ready to serve.

MAKE THE SLAW In a big bowl, combine both cabbages, the carrot, spring onions, and pineapple. In a separate bowl, whisk together the mayo, vinegar, granulated sugar (if using), salt, and pepper. Pour the dressing over the slaw, toss, and refrigerate until ready to serve.

To serve, mound as much of the pulled chicken and sauce on to each bun as you can handle, and top with some slaw.

Crispy Bacon
& Sweet Pickle
PATTY MELTS

By now I'm sure you know that I find food mash-ups to be a thing of absolute beauty. I go by the rule that if thing A is good and thing B is good then thing AB must be f*cking great. In this case, A is the cheese toastie you eat after 2 a.m. regrets and B is a Double Shackburger from Shake Shack.

The most patriotic I get is my love for American cheese. I actually just googled 'what is cheese' to see if American even fits the criteria for actual, authentic cheese and basically the only rule is that it must be derived from milk. That is literally the only rule. So to anyone that wants to question my love of American cheese, you can suck it! Don't challenge my patriotism.

SERVES 4
ACTIVE TIME / 20 MIN
TOTAL TIME / 25 MIN

½ medium yellow onion

350 g ground beef (preferably 80% lean)

5 slices bacon, cooked and finely crumbled

3 tablespoons sweet pickle relish

1 egg, lightly beaten

1 tablespoon finely minced garlic

1 teaspoon kosher salt

½ teaspoon freshly ground black pepper

½ teaspoon cayenne pepper

8 slices white bread

Butter, at room temperature

Vegetable oil

8 slices American-style cheese

Grate the onion into a bowl. Scoop up the grated onion with your hands and squeeze and discard the liquid. (You're going to wash your hands for the rest of the day. Sorry.) Return the squeezed onion to the bowl and add the beef, bacon, relish, egg, garlic, salt, black pepper and cayenne. Mix it all together using your hands, but gently. Pat out 4 thin patties and you get extra credit if you get them equal in size to the bread.

Generously spread one side of each slice of bread with softened butter.

Heat a large, heavy-bottomed frying pan or griddle over medium-high heat. Grease the pan with oil and when you see it just start to smoke, cook the patties until browned and a crust forms, 2 to 3 minutes per side. Transfer to a plate.

Reduce the heat to medium and arrange 4 slices of bread, butter-side down, in the pan. Layer each with a slice of cheese, a burger patty, and another slice of cheese. Top with a final slice of bread butter-side up.

Cook, pressing down slightly once in a while, until the bread is golden brown, crisp, and toasty, 2 to 3 minutes per side. Serve hot.

Philly FRENCH DIP SANDWICHES

Some of the biggest arguments I start on Twitter are about who makes the best of a city's favourite cuisine. When I go to Kansas City, I ask about BBQ. When I go to Charleston, I ask about fried chicken. And when I go to Philly, of course I have to ask about cheesesteaks. And all-out Twitter war ensues. Philly people are so passionate about which cheesesteak is the best. They're all so convinced that the other side is ridiculous and has terrible taste. But maybe we're all right, guys, okay? I personally prefer my cheesesteak with Cheese Whiz. But my little sauce for this sandwich is a more . . . sophisticated . . . American cheese au jus? Whatever. I just wanna pour the jus on my sandwich and then dip it in cheese sauce, okay? I'm right about this. And if you disagree, you have terrible taste.

SERVES 4
ACTIVE TIME / 30 MIN
TOTAL TIME / 30 MIN

FOR THE CHEESE SAUCE

3 tablespoons butter

3 tablespoons plain flour

250 ml whole milk

6 slices American-style cheese, torn into pieces

½ teaspoon kosher salt

⅛ teaspoon cayenne pepper

FOR THE STEAK

560 g sirloin steak, trimmed of excess fat, chilled in the freezer for 30 minutes

2 teaspoons soy sauce

Kosher salt and freshly ground black pepper

60 ml extra-virgin olive oil

1 jumbo onion, thinly sliced

4 cloves garlic, thinly sliced

250 ml beef stock

4 sub rolls

MAKE THE CHEESE SAUCE In a small heavy saucepan, heat the butter until foamy. Add the flour and cook, stirring, until blonde, 2 to 3 minutes. Whisk in the milk gradually and bring to a boil, reduce the heat, and simmer until thickened slightly, 3 to 4 minutes. Add the cheese, salt and cayenne and stir until smooth. Remove from the heat and cover to keep warm. (Reheat over low heat, if necessary, when you're about ready to serve.)

MAKE THE STEAK Remove the steak from the freezer and slice it really thinly against the grain. Place it in a bowl and toss it with the soy sauce and season generously with salt and pepper.

In a large frying pan, heat the oil over high heat. Add the onion and cook, stirring, until browned in spots and softened, about 9 minutes. Season with salt. Add the garlic and cook 1 additional minute. Add the meat and cook, stirring, until just cooked through and tender, 2 to 4 minutes. Transfer the meat and onions to a plate and cover to keep warm. Add the stock to the pan and bring to a boil, scraping up the browned bits on the bottom into the stock. Reduce the heat to medium and boil to reduce the liquid slightly to make a jus, about 4 minutes.

Split and toast the buns. Warm the beef jus over a very low flame. Divide the steak mixture among the bottom side of the buns and drizzle the jus evenly over the meat (just enough to moisten but not so much that the buns fall apart when you pick them up). Close the buns, cut them in half and serve them with the cheese sauce, dipping as you eat.

FRIED CHICKEN TOASTS
with Mashed Peas & Ricotta

A skinless boneless chicken boob has traditionally been a sad, lonely outcast in our fridge when there's a juicy thigh or a leg around . . . until now. The crunchy fried bread, the bed of creamy ricotta-pea mash, the crispy shallot topping that you make in the microwave (whaaaat?), the minty dressing . . . it's an open-faced sammy you might as well call Chrissy & John's Home for Orphaned Chicken Breasts. All boobs welcome.

SERVES 2
ACTIVE TIME / 15 MIN
TOTAL TIME / 45 MIN

FOR THE MASHED PEAS AND RICOTTA

55 g frozen peas, well thawed

125 g whole-milk ricotta cheese

Finely grated zest of ½ lemon

1 tablespoon Shallot Oil (page 130)

1 tablespoon finely shredded fresh mint

Kosher salt and freshly ground black pepper

FOR THE DRESSING

3 tablespoons Shallot Oil (page 130)

1 tablespoon fresh lemon juice

½ teaspoon Dijon mustard

Kosher salt and freshly ground black pepper

FOR THE CHICKEN AND TOASTS

1 boneless, skinless chicken breast

3 tablespoons Shallot Oil (page 130)

Kosher salt and freshly ground black pepper

2 big slices baguette

FOR SERVING

Kosher salt and freshly ground black pepper

Crispy Shallots (page 130)

A big pinch fresh mint, for garnish

A big pinch grated lemon zest, for garnish

MAKE THE MASHED PEAS AND RICOTTA In a medium bowl, combine the peas, ricotta, lemon zest, shallot oil, mint and salt and pepper to taste. Mash with a potato masher until chunky-creamy.

MAKE THE DRESSING In a screw-top jar, combine the shallot oil, lemon juice, mustard and salt and pepper to taste. Shake to combine.

FRY THE CHICKEN AND TOASTS Preheat a frying pan over medium-high heat.

Brush the chicken with 1 tablespoon of the shallot oil and season with salt and pepper. Fry until cooked through, 4 to 5 minutes per side. Remove to a plate, cool slightly, and slice against the grain into 5-mm-thick slices.

Brush each slice of bread with 1 tablespoon of the shallot oil and fry the toasts until golden, 2 to 3 minutes, flipping occasionally so the bread doesn't burn. Season the oiled side with salt and pepper.

TO SERVE Divide the mashed peas between the 2 toasts, then fan half the chicken on top of each toast. Season with more salt and pepper. Drizzle with the dressing, top with crispy shallots, and garnish with mint and lemon zest.

SNACKS

Crispy **COCONUT CHICKEN GOUJONS** with Pineapple-Chilli Sauce

I know. 'Chrissy, how do you come up with such genius things?' is what you are saying. Well, the answer is sometimes I just walk through the grocery store, see something in the frozen food aisle, and wonder why I can't make it at home. Then I do it. Or sometimes I pick something I love, like coconut shrimp, and say, 'Sh*t, I only have chicken,' and I make it. Geniuses work in all sorts of ways. Don't question my process.

SERVES 4 TO 6
ACTIVE TIME / 30 MIN
TOTAL TIME / 30 MIN
(plus up to 4 hrs marinating time)

FOR THE CHICKEN AND MARINADE

- **110 ml Thai sweet chilli sauce**
- **110 ml full-fat coconut milk, shaken**
- **110 ml pineapple juice (drained from a small can of crushed pineapple)**
- **Grated zest and juice of 1 lime**
- **3 cloves garlic, minced**
- **½ teaspoon kosher salt**
- **675 g chicken breast**

FOR THE SWEET CHILLI PINEAPPLE SAUCE

- **110 ml Thai sweet chilli sauce**
- **55 g canned crushed pineapple**
- **Grated zest and juice of 1 lime**
- **½ clove garlic, finely minced**
- **½ teaspoon Sriracha**

FOR BREADING AND FRYING

- **185 g cornflour (or flour if you don't have any cornflour)**
- **3 eggs**
- **80 g unsweetened shredded coconut**
- **50 g panko bread crumbs**
- **½ teaspoon cayenne pepper**
- **Kosher salt and freshly ground black pepper**
- **Vegetable oil, for shallow-frying**
- **2 spring onions, chopped, for garnish**

MARINATE THE CHICKEN In a large bowl, whisk together the sweet chilli sauce, coconut milk, pineapple juice, lime zest, lime juice, garlic, and salt. Slice the chicken into goujons and smush it around to coat. Cover and refrigerate for at least 30 minutes and up to 4 hours.

MAKE THE SAUCE In a small bowl, stir together the sweet chilli sauce, pineapple, lime zest, lime juice, garlic and Sriracha.

BREAD AND FRY THE CHICKEN Remove the chicken from the marinade, shaking off the excess liquid (discard the marinade). Set up three shallow bowls. Spread out the cornflour in one, beat the eggs in the second, and mix together the coconut, panko, cayenne, and 1 teaspoon salt and some black pepper in the third. Dip each chicken goujon in the cornflour, then in egg, shaking off the excess between each step. Press all sides of each tender into the coconut-panko mixture, pressing well to adhere, and place the breaded goujons on a plate or tray.

Heat 5 mm of oil in a large heavy frying pan over medium-high heat until hot. Working in batches, fry the goujons until golden and crisp, about 1½ minutes per side. Drain on paper towels and season to taste with salt. (You may need to add a little oil to the pan between batches of chicken to maintain the depth.)

Arrange the goujons on a serving platter and either serve with the sauce as a dip or drizzle them with the sauce. Garnish with spring onions and serve immediately.

Fried Thai-Glazed
CHICKEN WINGS

I'd like to start by first acknowledging the absolute best chicken wings in the world: David Chang's smoked chicken wings at Momofuku Noodle Bar in NYC. They're . . . unreal. They made me realize any good, saucy chicken wing MUST have a side of rice to pile said wings on top of. You then end up with a sort of sweet, salty dessert rice at the end. It's quite heavenly.

These guys are my own little version, with WAY less work.

I've been making this savoury/sweet/coconutty/citrusy marinade for a long, long time now. The sugar, once fried, gives each wing a special little birthmark of yum. Serve these with Tangy Herb-Sesame Slaw (page 68), or over the coconut rice recipe from *Cravings* 1.

SERVES 4 TO 6
ACTIVE TIME / 25 MIN
TOTAL TIME / 30 MIN
(plus up to 24 hrs marinating time)

1 (400-ml) can full-fat coconut milk, shaken

6 tablespoons fish sauce

6 tablespoons light brown sugar

2 tablespoons sesame oil

2 tablespoons chopped lemongrass (from 1 stalk; see Tip)

Grated zest and juice of 2 limes

10 small fresh Thai bird's eye chillies (hottt!) or 1 large jalapeño, chopped (or to taste)

2 teaspoons kosher salt

1.35 kg chicken wings, separated at the joint into sections

Chopped fresh coriander, for garnish

In a large bowl, combine the coconut milk, fish sauce, brown sugar, sesame oil, lemongrass, lime zest, lime juice, chillies and salt. Add the wings, toss to coat, cover, and marinate in the refrigerator for at least 4 hours and up to 24 hours.

Preheat a frying pan over medium-high heat. Remove the wings from the marinade and fry until the skin is crisp and golden, flipping once, 12 to 14 minutes total. Transfer to a serving platter and garnish with coriander.

Tip / *HOW TO PREP LEMONGRASS*

Peel the dry, outer layers of the lemongrass stalk until you see the bottom is a smooth, creamy colour. Finely chop just the white and very light-coloured part, about the bottom one-third of each stalk. That's the good stuff.

ONION DIP & Oven-Baked POTATO CRISPS

I hate saying it, but I have a glam squad. (It is literally my job to have a glam squad.) If you have seen me out and I am not wearing my hair in a top-knot, it means I have been sitting in a chair for 2½ hours getting head-to-toe makeup (yes, toe, seriously) and my extension-filled locks have been blown and braided to perfection.

What does this have to do with onion dip, you ask? Well, the number one rule of glam-chair: Do not eat anything of stench. I, of course, love my squad, but I am also a fierce rule breaker, so the first time I ever snacked on this onion dip was in that very chair. Of course, I forced everyone around me to try it as well, so as to not live a solo life of stench.

Glam people are very . . . glam. Gluten-free-vegan-nothing-above-20-degrees-raw-no-nightshades-or-sugar-or-salt-or-flavour types.

Those people ate the sh*t out of this dip.

SERVES 6 TO 8
(makes 500 ml dip and a whole pile of crisps)
ACTIVE TIME / 15 MIN
TOTAL TIME / 1 HR 25 MIN,
(includs chilling)

FOR THE DIP
- **2 tablespoons vegetable oil**
- **1 medium onion, finely chopped**
- **1 teaspoon kosher salt**
- **1 teaspoon freshly ground black pepper**
- **250 ml sour cream**
- **85 ml mayonnaise**
- **3 tablespoons finely chopped chives, plus more for garnish**
- **1½ teaspoons garlic powder**

FOR THE CHIPS
- **2 medium King Edward potatoes (about 450 g total)**
- **3 tablespoons olive oil**
- **1 teaspoon kosher salt**
- **1 teaspoon freshly ground black pepper, or more to taste**

MAKE THE DIP In a medium frying pan, heat the oil over medium-high heat. Add the onion and cook, stirring, for 5 minutes. Reduce the heat to medium-low, add ½ teaspoon each of the salt and pepper, and cook, stirring, until the onion is golden and caramelized, 15 more minutes. Remove from the heat and transfer to a bowl. Let cool for 10 minutes.

Add the sour cream, mayonnaise, chives, garlic powder, and the remaining ½ teaspoon each salt and pepper and stir to combine. Chill for at least 1 hour to let the flavours meld. The onion dip can be made up to 3 days ahead; keep refrigerated.

MAKE THE CHIPS Position racks in the top and bottom thirds of the oven and preheat the oven to 375°F/190°C. Line two large baking sheets with parchment paper.*

Slice the potatoes on a mandoline** into thin-as-a-penny slices. Pat the potatoes dry between two layers of paper towels, then toss them in a large bowl with the olive oil, salt and pepper. Really use your hands to rub them to make sure the slices get coated in the oil and aren't stuck to each other.

Separate the slices and arrange them*** on the lined baking sheets. Bake until golden and crisp, switching racks and rotating the pans front to back halfway through, 12 to 15 minutes (the chips will bake at different rates; the small ones will bake first, so watch 'em). You'll know when they're done because they'll have gotten a little wavy, lifted themselves off the pan, and turned browned in spots. And the potatoes may seem to colour unevenly, but they will still be crispy when cooled. Remove from the oven, cool, and serve with the dip.

★ / Of course, you could always use a deep fryer and ditch the baking sheets! If so, fill a pot halfway with vegetable oil (not olive), heat over medium-heat until one slice of potato dropped into the oil sizzles immediately, and fry the chips in batches until golden brown and crispy, 1 to 2 minutes per batch. Drain on paper towels, then salt and pepper the f*ck out of 'em.

★★ / If you don't have a mandoline (or are just into fingertip preservation), use a really sharp knife to cut the potatoes.

★★★ / If you have potato slices that really vary in diameter, arrange all the small ones on one sheet and the big ones on the other so they cook evenly. You may end up pulling the small ones a minute or two earlier than the big ones.

CHICKEN NACHOS
with Avocado Salsa

These are nachos with BBQ chicken. They're the sh*t.
What else can I say, they're nachos.

1 bag tortilla chips

250 g pulled chicken (from
   Pulled BBQ Chicken
   Sandwiches with
   Pineapple Slaw, page 83)

450 g shredded pepper Jack
   cheese, or more if you
   want

FOR THE SALSA
2 large avocados, diced

1 small red onion, finely diced

1 tomato, diced

2 tablespoons chopped fresh
   coriander

Grated zest and juice of 1 lime

Kosher salt and freshly
   ground black pepper

FOR THE TOPPING
Sour cream

Sliced fresh or pickled
   jalapeños

Fresh coriander

Preheat the oven to 375°F/190°C.

Arrange the chips on a large rimmed baking sheet in a
single layer. Top with the pulled chicken and then the
pepper Jack cheese. Bake until the cheese is bubbling
and the edges of the chips are crisp, 20 to 25 minutes.

MEANWHILE, MAKE THE SALSA In a large bowl,
gently toss together the avocados, onion, tomato,
coriander, lime zest, lime juice, and salt and pepper
to taste.

Remove the nachos from the oven and top with the
salsa, sour cream, jalapeños, and coriander.

SERVES 6 TO 8
ACTIVE TIME / 40 MIN
TOTAL TIME / 2 HRS 30 MIN

Mushroom & Crispy Shallot
NACHOS

I could show off this chip stack to you as a way of showing off a new, trying-to-eat-less-meat Chrissy, but then you'd know I was lying and you'd call B.S. on me, and *then* I'd have to block you on (insert social media platform). The truth is, mushrooms are like earth's candy to me, and sliced up and cooked and piled between layers of crunchy chips and spicy, stretchy, gooey cheese . . . be gone, cow. You aren't needed. Today.

SERVES 6
ACTIVE TIME / 45 MIN
TOTAL TIME / 1 HR

- **4 tablespoons rapeseed oil**
- **1 large onion, thinly sliced**
- **3 cloves garlic, thinly sliced**
- **450–550 g mushrooms, trimmed and thinly sliced**
- **1 tablespoon chilli powder**
- **½ teaspoon dried oregano**
- **½ teaspoon cayenne pepper**
- **Kosher salt and freshly ground black pepper**

- **1 large bag tortilla chips**
- **135 g shredded pepper Jack cheese**
- **135 g shredded sharp white cheddar cheese**
- **1 large jalapeño (red or green), chopped (seeded if you want it less hot)**
- **1 tomato, seeded and diced**
- **2 spring onions, thinly sliced**
- **Crispy Shallots (page 130)**

Preheat the oven to 375°F/190°C.

In a large frying pan, heat 2 tablespoons of the oil over medium heat. Add the onion and cook, stirring, until golden, 9 to 10 minutes. Add the garlic and cook 1 additional minute. Scoop it out on to a plate.

Add the remaining 2 tablespoons oil, then add the mushrooms, increase the heat to medium-high, and cook, stirring, until the mushrooms release their water, about 7 minutes. Add the chilli powder, oregano, cayenne, ½ teaspoon salt and ¼ teaspoon black pepper and cook 1 additional minute. Stir the onions into the mushroom mixture. Add more salt and pepper to taste.

Scatter the chips on a large rimmed baking sheet. Scatter the onion-mushroom mixture on top of the chips, then top with the cheeses and half the jalapeños. Bake until the cheese is melted and bubbling, about 15 minutes. Remove from the oven and scatter with the remaining jalapeños, the tomato, spring onions, and plenty of crispy shallots. Serve right away.

Hollowed-Out
ITALIAN SANDWICH

I still remember the moment I created this beast and made enough to pass around the Ford Amphitheater during a Chrissy Teigen's Husband show. One of my dreams is to have a picnic basket company. Beautiful baskets packed with custom-made-with-love goodies for lovers or families to munch on at the park or on long road trips to stalk your ex. This sandwich will be the first thing I stuff in that basket. I'm actually eight months pregnant now and apparently consuming deli meats is comparable to snorting meth in pregnancy-world so it is PAINFUL for me to talk about how freakin' good this sandwich is. I crave NOTHING more than I crave this sandwich. Layers of artichokes, peppers, and fancy pants bologna. Get a nice loaf and slather on the mayo without a care in the world. THIS IS TORTURE.

SERVES 6 TO 8
ACTIVE TIME / 20 MIN
TOTAL TIME / 2 HRS 30 MIN

FOR THE ROASTED GARLIC MAYO

15 cloves Stovetop Roasted Garlic (recipe follows)

125 ml mayonnaise

1 tablespoon Dijon mustard

¼ teaspoon freshly ground black pepper

Kosher salt

FOR THE SANDWICH

1 round sourdough loaf

250-300 g sliced provolone, mozzarella, or any cheese you want

1 (340-g) jar roasted peppers, drained and patted dry

175-225 g thinly sliced mortadella

175-225 g thinly sliced salami

1 (340 g) jar marinated artichoke hearts, drained (but NOT rinsed), and finely chopped

4 whole pickled pepperoncini (available online), patted dry and sliced

10 basil leaves

Kosher salt and freshly ground black pepper

MAKE THE MAYO Combine the garlic, mayo, mustard and pepper in a cup and whizz with a stick blender until smooth (or chop the roasted garlic really small and mix it in a bowl). Season with salt to taste.

MAKE THE SANDWICH Cut off the top 5 cm or so of the bread. Hollow out the bread, scooping out the insides with your hands and making sure to leave about 3 cm on the sides and bottom so it can hold the fillings. Reserve the bread insides for another purpose, like bread crumbs (see page 178).

Spread the inside of the hollowed-out bread generously with the roasted garlic mayo, but save some for the top, too. Then start layering your ingredients: a layer of cheese, a layer of roasted peppers, some of the meats, half the chopped artichokes and pepperoncini, seasoning the vegetables with salt and pepper and throwing in the basil leaves wherever you like. Fill up the bread with as much meat, cheese, peppers, artichokes and pepperoncini as it can hold. Make sure the sandwich is really packed with the fillings, pressing down with your hands if you need to make room for more layers. Spread the reserved bread top with the rest of the roasted garlic mayo and press the top on to the fillings so it just looks like the original round loaf. Wrap the whole thing tightly in plastic wrap and let it sit for 2 hours (put it in the fridge if you're going to let it hang out for longer than that). Cut into wedges and serve.

Stovetop Roasted Garlic & Garlic Oil

**MAKES ABOUT 400 G
GARLIC CLOVES AND
500 ML OIL
ACTIVE TIME / 10 MIN
TOTAL TIME / 50 MIN**

This recipe is also in my first book, but if you don't already have it, I'm going to include it here because you need it in your life.

540 ml olive oil

30 large or 40 medium cloves peeled garlic

Combine the oil and garlic in a small saucepan. Turn the heat on medium-low and let the oil heat up slowly. The garlic will sizzle after 10 or 15 minutes. Cook the garlic until it turns golden brown but stays really soft, 30 to 40 minutes longer (if it gets dark or develops a bubbly, sort-of-hard outer layer, turn the heat down).

Turn off the heat and let the garlic cool in the oil. Strain the garlic from the oil and keep each one refrigerated separately in tightly sealed containers. Before using the oil, let it come to room temperature or put the jar in a bowl of warm water for 1 minute to liquefy if need be.

King's Hawaiian Pull-Apart
BACON CHEESE TOASTIES

LOL this recipe's name is so bonkers. It's insane. I love this book. Anyhow, every time I open up a package of King's Hawaiian rolls, I fall in love with the soft, 3 × 4 pillow of sweet, golden brown bread. My first inclination is to rip off a square and shove it into my mouth but one day, one rare day of patience, apparently, I thought to myself, 'Why not keep these suckers all stuck together and slice them all right through their midsections?' Now, I normally only have good ideas, but this one? This one was great.

The four-cheese combo ensures an extremely Snapchatable stretch of cheese. Am I going to cringe that I wrote that ten years from now? Definitely. Who cares.

MAKES 12 MINI
SANDWICHES
ACTIVE TIME / 15 MIN
TOTAL TIME / 25 MIN

1 pack of 12 soft mini burger buns or King's Hawaiian original sweet rolls (available online)

Vegetable oil, for brushing

150 g whipped or spreadable cream cheese

Kosher salt and freshly ground black pepper

115 g shredded Gouda cheese

115 g shredded cheddar cheese

115 g shredded pepper Jack cheese

6 slices bacon, cooked and crumbled (optional)

2 tablespoons Dijon mustard

1 tablespoon Hot Honey (page 225) or regular honey

Place two baking sheets in the oven and preheat it to 375°F/190°C.

While you're preheating, brush the underside of the entire connected sheet of rolls with vegetable oil, then place the whole thing on a cutting board. Using a serrated knife, carefully slice horizontally through the batch of rolls to create a top and a bottom sheet. Spread the inside of the bottom sheet with the cream cheese, season with salt and pepper, and sprinkle the shredded cheeses evenly all over the sheet. Sprinkle the crumbled bacon, if using, over the cheeses.

Spread the inside of the top sheet of rolls with the mustard and drizzle with the honey, then place it on the bottom sheet to form one giant sandwich (the rolls should all still be connected on each sheet).

Using an oven mitt, remove one baking sheet from the oven (it's hot!!) and transfer the sandwich to the middle of the sheet (using two hands and moving the thing in one confident motion is the best way here). With the oven mitt, remove the second sheet from the oven and centre it on top of the sandwich – you want to squash the sandwich a little bit. Weight the top sheet down with something heavy and ovenproof, like a large pan. Transfer the whole thing back to the oven and bake until the cheese is melted, the underside is golden, and the top is toasty, 9 to 10 minutes.

Transfer the sandwich to a platter and serve hot. Pulling the little sandwiches apart with your hands is the most fun, but you can slice them with a serrated knife, too.

Peanut Butter Pretzel
GRANOLA CLUSTERS

It's John here. I'm writing about this because I'm in love with peanut butter and this snack takes me to my happy place. I've loved peanut butter since I was a kid - I used to sneak my fingers into the peanut butter jar, and when my mom would discover the finger marks in the peanut butter, she would line up me and my three siblings for an interrogation to determine the culprit. I was foolish enough to lie about it, not realizing that the smell of peanut butter still lingered in my mouth. I got in trouble, not for eating the peanut butter but for lying about it. Don't you hate when parents say that? 'It's not that you did it; it's that you lied about it!' I'm totally gonna say that to Luna. Anyhow, peanut butter tastes great with granola! Enjoy!

MAKES 350 G
ACTIVE TIME / 5 MIN
TOTAL TIME / 20 MIN

- 175 g peanut butter chips or smooth peanut butter
- 125 g Salted Maple Granola (page 40)
- 60 g roughly crushed salted mini pretzels

Line a baking sheet with foil. In a medium saucepan, heat the peanut butter chips until melted and smooth, about 3 minutes, or just warm the peanut butter. Add the granola and pretzels and stir until coated. Transfer to the lined baking sheet and freeze for 15 minutes. Break into clusters. Store in the fridge for up to 2 weeks.

Fluffy CORN DOGS

Corn dogs: where you basically get a piece of cake wrapped around one of the world's most perfect foods, stuck on a stick, and puffed up in oil. *Yesss.* Why don't people make them at home? Do you *want* to have to wait for your once-a-year state fair before your next corn dog? Make a corn dog at home. And it's SOOOO much better at home: piping hot and perfectly crispy. Sh*t, that's a good book title. Be on the lookout for *Cravings 3: Piping Hot and Perfectly Crispy.*

MAKES 8
ACTIVE TIME / 15 MIN
TOTAL TIME / 30 MIN

Vegetable oil, for deep-frying

150 g polenta

90 g plain flour, plus more for dredging the hot dogs

25 g sugar

4 teaspoons baking powder

1 teaspoon kosher salt

½ teaspoon cayenne pepper

310 ml buttermilk, plus more if needed

1 egg, lightly beaten

8 hot dogs

8 thick wooden skewers or wooden chopsticks

Hot Chinese mustard (or mustard of your choice)

Pour 130 mm of oil into a large pot and heat over medium heat to 360°F/180°C. (Use a deep-fry thermometer or test the oil by throwing in a little piece of bread or some bread crumbs; if they sizzle immediately but aren't burning, you're ready.)

In a large bowl, whisk together the polenta, flour, sugar, baking powder, salt and cayenne. Add the buttermilk and egg and stir with a spoon until a thick batter forms (it will be much thicker than pancake batter). Scrape the batter with a spatula into a tall drinking glass (you can also put it in a wide, shallowish bowl). Chill for 15 minutes (this helps the batter adhere to the dog and not slip off when it hits the oil).

Put some flour on a plate. Pat the hot dogs dry with paper towels, and run a skewer through each lengthwise, making sure to leave enough for a handle. Roll the hot dogs in the flour and shake off the excess. One at a time, dip the hot dogs into the glass of batter to coat completely, including the bottom where the hot dog meets the stick. (If using a bowl, spin the hot dog in the batter to coat all over.) Shake off some of the excess, twirling the hot dog at the same time to keep the batter uniform. As you work, if the batter gets too thick, add a splash of buttermilk (but don't add too much or the batter won't cling to the dogs!).

Three or four at a time, gently drop the coated dogs into the oil, making sure not to move them so the batter sets around the dogs and fry until nice and deep golden and crisp, turning once during cooking, 4 to 5 minutes. Drain on paper towels and serve hot with mustard.

POTATOES & THEIR FRIENDS

Crispy POTATO SMASHIES

Just when I thought I'd had potatoes EVERY way humanly possible, I stumbled upon these. And they have totally screwed up my 'favourite way to eat potatoes' ranking system. Now I dunno where anything freakin' goes any more. And why did it take me so long to find these??? You can serve them as hors d'oeuvres, perhaps with a little dollop of sour cream and fresh chives on top, or do like the Teigens and toss 'em in a bowl and go to town on them with a rib eye. This is assuming you don't eat them straight off the baking sheet, which is also a very Teigen thing to do.

SERVES 6
ACTIVE TIME / 5 MIN
TOTAL TIME / 50 MIN

675 g baby potatoes (the smallest you can find: 16 to 24 potatoes)

60 ml olive oil

1½ teaspoons kosher salt

1 teaspoon freshly ground black pepper, or more to taste

2 tablespoons chopped fresh flat-leaf parsley

Preheat the oven to 425°F/220°C. (If using an electric oven, see Note.)

Put the potatoes in a large microwave-safe bowl and fill the bottom with ½ inch of water. Cover with plastic wrap and poke the wrap a few times with a fork. Microwave on high until the potatoes can be easily pierced with a fork, somewhere between 15 and 20 minutes (check after 10 minutes; if they're still hard, return them for another 5, and so on, replenishing the water, if necessary). Remove, uncover, drain well and cool until just warm.

Using the heel of your hand, smash the potatoes into rounds. (You want them to hold together, so be gentle. Love your potatoes, even when you're smashing them in the face.)

Pour the oil on to a large rimmed baking sheet and sprinkle the oil with ¾ teaspoon of the salt and ½ teaspoon of the pepper. Arrange the smashies on the sheet and sprinkle the tops with the remaining ¾ teaspoon salt and ½ teaspoon pepper. Put it on the *floor* of the oven (yep) and roast until the undersides are crispy but not burnt, 10 to 15 minutes. Remove the pan from the oven and use tongs or a spatula to flip the potatoes, then return to the oven and roast until the undersides are crispy, another 10 to 15 minutes. Remove from the oven, transfer to a serving platter, and garnish with the parsley.

Note / ELECTRIC AVENUE

If you're making these in an electric oven, position a rack as close to the heating coil as possible and preheat to 425°F/220°C. Microwave and smash the potatoes as directed. Place a large rimmed baking sheet into the oven until water sizzles when sprinkled on the surface, about 5 minutes. Remove the hot sheet from the oven, pour the oil on to it, sprinkle it with ¾ teaspoon of the salt and ½ teaspoon of the pepper, then quickly arrange the smashies on the sheet and sprinkle with the remaining ¾ teaspoon salt and ½ teaspoon pepper. Roast and serve as directed.

Crispy
BUFFALO SMASHIES

Plain CPS (Crispy Potato Smashies, duh) are a sidepiece. Buffalo Blue Cheese CPS? Party snack on a Guy Fieri acid trip train to Flavourtown.

SERVES 6
ACTIVE TIME / 15 MIN
TOTAL TIME / 50 MIN

**Crispy Potato Smashies
(page 116)**

FOR THE BLUE
CHEESE SAUCE

185 ml sour cream

**60 g crumbled blue
cheese**

**2 tablespoons
mayonnaise**

**2 tablespoons
buttermilk, shaken**

**Freshly ground black
pepper**

FOR THE BUFFALO
SAUCE

3 tablespoons butter

**1 clove garlic, finely
minced**

**60 ml Frank's RedHot
sauce**

**¼ teaspoon cayenne
pepper**

**Freshly ground black
pepper**

**Chopped chives, for
garnish**

Make the smashies as directed. While the potatoes are roasting, make the two sauces.

MAKE THE BLUE CHEESE SAUCE In a small bowl, whisk together the sour cream, blue cheese, mayo, buttermilk and black pepper to taste.

MAKE THE BUFFALO SAUCE In a small saucepan, heat the butter and garlic over medium-high heat until the butter melts and the garlic is fragrant, about 2 minutes. (Or you can microwave them together for 45 seconds to 1½ minutes.) Whisk in the hot sauce, cayenne and black pepper to taste and return to the heat just to warm it back up. Cover to keep warm.

ASSEMBLE THE POTATOES When the potatoes are done, remove them from the oven and dump them on to a serving platter. Pour the warm Buffalo sauce (reheat it if you need to) over the potatoes and drizzle with the blue cheese sauce. Season to taste with black pepper and garnish with chives.

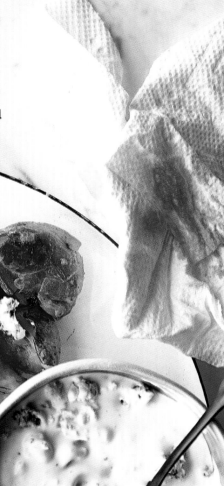

Crispy-Coated Oven-Roasted SWEET POTATO WEDGES

I've been pretty vocal in the past about my hatred of sweet potato fries.

Okay, so maybe I wasn't ballsy enough to say I hate them, but man, did I hate them. I just didn't ever feel like they were capable of being anything more than, 'Meh, these are edible with some sauce,' which is not acceptable if you're setting yourself up to be compared to French fries.

But with persistence comes success. (I don't know if that's a saying, but it sounds like one.) I present to you these beautifully thick, salty, crispy-on-the-outside and soft-n-sweet-on-the-inside Lawry's sweet potato wedges. For anyone outside of the US, Lawry's make the best seasoned salt, and no, they have not paid me for this prime book placement, so use whatever seasoning salt you want. Seriously though, Lawry's is damn good.

SERVES 4 TO 6
ACTIVE TIME / 10 MIN
TOTAL TIME / 40 MIN

3 tablespoons olive oil

2 egg whites

2 tablespoons rice flour (see Note)

2 teaspoons seasoned salt, plus more for sprinkling

675 g smallish sweet potatoes, skin on, cut lengthwise into 2-cm-thick wedges

Preheat the oven to 425°F/220°C. Place the oil on a large rimmed baking sheet and heat it in the oven until very hot but not smoking, 7 to 8 minutes.

Hand-whisk the egg whites in a large bowl until stiff peaks form, about 4 minutes. (Or use an electric mixer fitted with the whisk attachment and reduce the time to about 2 minutes.) Gently fold in the rice flour and seasoned salt, then gently toss the potatoes in the egg white mixture.

Using an oven mitt, remove the baking sheet from the oven and quickly arrange the coated potato wedges on the hot oil, making sure a flat side of each potato is coming into direct contact with the oil. Roast until the undersides are crispy, 13 to 15 minutes. Flip the wedges with tongs and roast until the other side is golden, 10 to 15 minutes. Remove from the oven and sprinkle with additional salt if desired.

Note / *GETTING RICE FLOUR (OR NOT)*

You can find rice flour in a lot of stores, but if you can't, go for cornflour or potato starch.

Two-Tone
POTATO GRATIN

This is one of those recipes that was on my blog (may she rest in peace) and you haven't. stopped. asking. for. it. As you may recall, it was part of a giant Thanksgiving menu, and I am famous (infamous? whichever one is the bad one) for making *all* of the food, then falling asleep before it even got served. So consider yourselves lucky I stayed up long enough to write this recipe down. Now excuse me while I just close my eyes for a hot minute. . . .

SERVES 10 TO 12
ACTIVE TIME / 30 MIN
TOTAL TIME / 1 HR 30 MIN

685 ml double heavy cream

3 cloves garlic, finely minced

1 tablespoon chopped fresh thyme, or 1 teaspoon dried, plus fresh thyme for garnish

1 tablespoon chopped fresh sage, or 1 teaspoon dried

1 teaspoon chopped fresh or dried rosemary

2 teaspoons kosher salt

1 teaspoon freshly ground black pepper

¼ teaspoon grated nutmeg

Dash of cayenne pepper

200 g shredded Gruyère cheese

160 g finely grated Parmigiano-Reggiano cheese

900 g sweet potatoes

675 g King Edward potatoes

Preheat the oven to 425°F/220°C.

In a large bowl, whisk together the cream, garlic, thyme, sage, rosemary, salt, black pepper, nutmeg and cayenne. In a separate bowl, toss together the Gruyère and Parm.

Peel the potatoes, then with a handheld mandoline or a sharp knife, slice the potatoes crosswise into 3-mm-thick rounds. Pour 125 ml of the cream mixture into a 23 × 33-cm baking dish, then make a layer of potatoes in as nice a pattern as you can, overlapping the slices slightly. (You can do this in individual layers of sweet potatoes and regular potatoes, or mix them up, or do all the sweet and then all the regular . . . basically, you do you!) Drizzle 185 ml of the cream mixture on top and sprinkle with 115 g of the cheese mixture. Repeat this layering two more times. Finish with a top layer of potatoes and sprinkle the remaining cheese on top of that. Garnish with fresh thyme.

Cover with foil and bake until bubbling, about 30 minutes. Remove the foil, reduce the oven temperature to 400°F/200°C, and bake until the top is golden and bubbling, another 30 minutes. Turn the oven to grill, or pop it under a hot grill until the top is browned, 1 to 2 minutes.

Note / *DRIED HERBS ARE YOUR FRIENDS*

In most cases, you can swap in dried herbs for fresh – just use one-third the amount of dried herbs as you would fresh. So if a recipe calls for 3 teaspoons (or 1 tablespoon, because those are the same thing!!) chopped fresh thyme, replace it with 1 teaspoon dried. If I'm honest, I do usually like the taste of fresh herbs better. But when I stood there for like 30 minutes one day picking thyme for a recipe from my first book, I thought, 'Why the hell did I make people stand there for 30 minutes picking thyme?'

Salt-&-Vinegar
BAKED CHIPS

These are an edible optical illusion – they look like plain old chips, but a) they are baked! and b) bite into them and you get that sour salt-and-vinegar kick usually found only inside a bag of crisps. I'm all for less oil when you don't sacrifice the yum, and this is one of those cases. You have to boil them first to really get that distinctive mouth-puckering flavour all up inside, but baking them after their hot-water soak makes the outsides super crisp and the insides perfectly fluffy.

SERVES 4
ACTIVE TIME / 15 MIN
TOTAL TIME / 45 MIN

500 ml distilled white vinegar

50 g kosher salt, plus more for seasoning

8 large King Edward potatoes skin on, scrubbed

6 tablespoons vegetable oil

Finely chopped chives, for garnish

Preheat the oven to 450°F/230°C.

In a large pot, combine 1.5 litres water, the vinegar and kosher salt and bring to a boil over high heat.

Meanwhile, cut the potatoes: Stand each potato up on its long side and cut it lengthwise into 1-cm-thick ovals. Stack the ovals and cut them lengthwise into batons (basically, make chip shapes, OK?).

Line a baking sheet with kitchen towel. Put the potatoes into the water (it's OK if it's not boiling yet), bring to a boil, and boil for 8 minutes. Remove with a slotted spoon (be careful not to break them; they should still be sort of firm but bendy) to the lined baking sheet to soak up all the additional liquid. Spread the potatoes out in one layer and blot them dry with paper towels. Let cool.

Transfer the potatoes to a large bowl and toss with 2 tablespoons of the oil and 1 teaspoon salt. Divide the remaining 4 tablespoons oil between two large rimmed baking sheets (2 tablespoons per sheet).

Heat the oiled sheets in the oven until very hot but not smoking, 5 to 6 minutes. Using an oven mitt, remove the sheets from the oven and quickly divide the potatoes between them, making sure they all actually sit on the surface of the pan. Return to the oven and bake until the undersides are brown and crisp and the top edges are darkened, about 20 minutes. Open the oven, scrape the chips with a metal spatula to turn them, then bake until they are golden and crisp all around, another 10 minutes. Drain on paper towels and season with more salt. Garnish with chives.

TATERS, SHROOMS & PEAS
with Parmesan Cream

Aren't frozen peas just the best? They're sweet, they're perky, and they're always ready for a good time (are they on Tinder?). Please exit now if you even thought about popping fresh ones out of their little shell – swith peas, it's all about the bag. Besides, the potatoes (don't overcook 'em!) and mushrooms (hard to mess up) are fresh, so your foodie cred is covered. A little thyme combined with a not-so-little amount of double cream and Parm simmers into a sauce that coats those veggies like a blanket. Serve this with fried eggs for a simple meal.

SERVES 4 AS A SIDE DISH
OR 2 AS A MAIN DISH WITH
AN EGG ON TOP
ACTIVE TIME / 15 MIN
TOTAL TIME / 45 MIN

FOR THE PARMESAN CREAM

250 ml double cream

120 g finely grated Parmigiano-Reggiano cheese, plus more for garnish

½ teaspoon kosher salt

A few gratings of fresh nutmeg (about ⅛ teaspoon)

FOR THE VEGETABLES

450 g Yukon Gold or Desiree potatoes, skin on, scrubbed and cut into ½-inch cubes

4 tablespoons olive oil

225 g white mushrooms, trimmed and quartered

1 large shallot, thinly sliced

½ teaspoon dried thyme

1 tablespoon butter

150 g frozen peas

Kosher salt and freshly ground black pepper

MAKE THE PARMESAN CREAM In a small saucepan, bring the cream to a simmer over medium-low heat and reduce by half, about 5 minutes. Whisk in the Parm, salt and nutmeg. Cook 1 additional minute, whisking, then remove from the heat and cover to keep warm.

COOK THE VEGETABLES Place the potatoes in a microwave-safe bowl and add 1 cm of water to the bowl. Cover the bowl with a plate or plastic wrap, poke some holes in the plastic, and microwave on high until the potatoes can be pierced with a fork, 8 to 10 minutes (stop the microwave at 8 minutes to check the potatoes' progress). Drain the potatoes and set aside.

Meanwhile, in a large frying pan, heat 2 tablespoons of the oil over medium-high heat until hot but not smoking. Add the mushrooms, spread them out in one layer, and cook, without touching them, until they get a little golden, about 3 minutes. Add the remaining 2 tablespoons olive oil and the shallots and cook until translucent, about 2 minutes.

Add the potatoes and thyme and cook, stirring occasionally, until the potatoes turn a little golden, 6 to 7 minutes. Add the butter and peas and cook until the peas are heated through, about 3 minutes. Season to taste with salt and pepper (but remember that delicious salty Parm cream is gonna go in there too), cook for another minute to let the seasoning soak in, and transfer to a serving dish. Drizzle the Parmesan cream (start with about half and add more as desired) over the vegetables and gently toss. Season to taste with salt and pepper and garnish with some grated Parm.

Pepper's GRIDDLED AUBERGINE
with Crispy Shallots

As I've said before, Mom has a habit of making the most incredible stuff without *ever* writing it down (and with a Stella in hand), which means that no one else can ever really know what's in anything she's made . . . and neither does she. So I literally made my assistant, Christine, stand by her side with a notepad writing stuff down, since Mom and I fight when I try to do it because I realize how she's been a sneaky-sneak literally my entire life. All of the secrets come out, like, 'Oh, yes, I know I told you light soy sauce, but it's actually sweet soy sauce from Thai Town and, no, they don't sell it any more and I used the last of the bottle.' So my promise to you: Everything you need to make this killer sauce has not been discontinued or put on some do-not-import list. And you will like this aubergine even if you don't like aubergine. It's salted to make it soft and seasoned and absorb the sweet-savoury-garlicky sauce, and grilled because where there's smoke, there's flavour.

SERVES 4 TO 6
ACTIVE TIME / 15 MIN
TOTAL TIME / 45 MIN

2 large aubergines cut unto 2-cm-thick slices

Kosher salt

60 ml hoisin sauce

60 ml fresh lime juice (from 2 limes)

3 tablespoons sake*

2 tablespoons low-sodium soy sauce

1½ tablespoons Sriracha

4 teaspoons fish sauce

200 g light brown sugar

6 cloves garlic, finely minced

Rapeseed oil, for brushing

Crispy Shallots (recipe follows)

Chopped fresh coriander, for garnish

★ / Instead of sake you can use 1½ tablespoons each vodka and mirin (Japanese sweet cooking wine).

Arrange the aubergine slices on a rack set over a baking sheet. Sprinkle both sides with salt and let sit until they have released some of their liquid, about 30 minutes.

While the aubergine is just sitting there, make the sauce: In a small saucepan, combine the hoisin sauce, lime juice, sake, soy sauce, Sriracha, fish sauce, brown sugar and garlic. Bring to a boil, then reduce the heat and gently simmer until the sauce is reduced to about 250 ml, about 5 minutes. Transfer to a bowl to cool.

Pat the aubergine dry with paper towels. Moisten a paper towel lightly with rapeseed oil and use it to oil a griddle pan. Heat the pan over medium-high heat until very hot but not smoking. Brush both sides of the aubergine lightly with oil. Working in batches, griddle the aubergine until softened and griddle marks form, 6 to 7 minutes per side. Arrange the aubergine on a platter, drizzle the sauce on top, and garnish with the crispy shallots and coriander.

Crispy Shallots & Shallot Oil

100 g thinly sliced shallots
250 ml rapeseed oil
Kosher salt

Scatter the shallots evenly in a 20 × 20-cm glass dish. Pour the oil over the shallots and microwave on high until the shallots are browned and crisp, 6 to 8 minutes. (Begin checking them at 6 minutes as they can darken quickly.) Quickly and carefully drain the shallots in a fine-mesh sieve set over a bowl to catch the oil. Transfer the shallots to paper towels and season with salt. Let cool completely. The shallots will keep in an airtight container for a week. Store the oil in an airtight container in the fridge for up to 1 month.

MAKES ABOUT 250 ML OIL
ACTIVE TIME / 7 MIN
TOTAL TIME / 15 MIN

Golden Onion
RICE PILAF

I'd like to think I can cook with the best home cooks out there. I can braise, I can grill, I can fry, I can ferment, I can sauté, I can stir-fry. But I cannot . . . cook . . . rice. I have a hunch this has something to do with my love of vodka-sodas, because I seem to always get a little distracted before it becomes a burnt mess that must soak overnight in the sink.

But this rice is foolproof. Failproof. The timing is spot-on and it's near impossible to end up with it burnt OR mush-mush-times. Not to mention, I can't imagine what you wouldn't want to serve this buttery rice with. Or eat it by itself if you have zero shame like I do. I mean, I eat boxed stuffing by itself. The name is basically telling you to stuff it into something, anything, first, but nope: I'm f*ckin' doin' this.

MAKES ABOUT 5 CUPS /
SERVES 4
ACTIVE TIME / 15 MIN
TOTAL TIME / 50 MIN

225 g long-grain rice

2 tablespoons butter, plus butter pats for serving

2 tablespoons olive oil

1 large onion, finely diced

3 cloves garlic, finely minced

625 ml chicken or vegetable stock

2 teaspoons kosher salt

1 teaspoon freshly ground black pepper

1 lemon

Rinse the rice in a sieve under cold water until the water runs clear. Drain well. (Pat the bottom of the sieve to help get the water out.)

In a 3-litre saucepan, heat the butter and oil over medium heat. Add the onion and cook, stirring, until slightly golden and soft, 9 to 10 minutes (make sure the onion doesn't darken too much; that's not what you're going for here).

Add the garlic and cook, stirring, for 1 additional minute. Add the rice and cook, stirring, until the rice is shiny and translucent, 2 to 3 minutes. Add the stock, salt and pepper and bring to a boil. Reduce the heat to low for a very gentle simmer, cover, and let the rice cook without raising the lid (DFWI!!!) until the rice is cooked, about 18 minutes.

Use a microplane or other fine zester to zest the lemon into the rice to taste. Fluff and serve with pats of butter and wedges of the zested lemon.

Spicy Honey-Butter
CARROT COINS

This is . . . exactly what the title says it is.

SERVES 4
ACTIVE TIME / 10 MIN
TOTAL TIME / 30 MIN

**675 g carrots, peeled
and cut into ½-cm-
thick coins**

3 tablespoons butter

1½ tablespoons honey

**¼ teaspoon cayenne
pepper, plus more to
taste**

**Kosher salt and freshly
ground black pepper**

In a large saucepan, combine the carrots and 125 ml water, cover tightly, and set over medium heat. Cook the carrots without removing the lid for 15 minutes, checking after 10 to make sure there's still water in the pan. (If your lid doesn't fit super tight, check earlier; if it's dry on the bottom of the pan, add a couple tablespoons water.)

Uncover – the water should all be absorbed and the carrots may even be slightly golden underneath but not burnt. If there's any water left, drain it off. Reduce the heat to medium-low and add the butter, honey, cayenne, ½ teaspoon salt and ¼ teaspoon black pepper and cook, stirring the whole time, until the butter melts and the carrots are glazed, 2 to 3 minutes. Season with more cayenne and salt and pepper to taste.

Jalapeño-Cheddar
CORN PUDDING

If this sounds familiar, it's because it was part of the legendary Thanksgiving menu of 2015 from my blog (RIP). So if you've already made this, thank you for keeping my blog in your thoughts and prayers. And if you're making it for the first time, marvel at how the thing holds together like a fancy soufflé, because the cornflour binds everything together. (Did you know the secret ingredient in creamed corn is actually cornflour?) But, I mean, the several cups of melted cheese probably help bind everything together, too.

SERVES 8 TO 10
ACTIVE TIME / 15 MIN
TOTAL TIME / 1 HR

4 tablespoons butter, melted, plus more for the pan

2 tablespoons cornflour

185 ml double cream

200 g shredded cheddar cheese

2 (425-g) cans cream-style sweetcorn

Kernels from 2 large ears corn (or one 425 g can sweetcorn, drained)

2 large or 4 small seeded diced jalapeños

6 eggs

Kosher salt

Preheat the oven to 350°F/175°C. Grease a 23 × 333-cm baking pan with butter.

In a large bowl, whisk the cornflour into the double cream until smooth. Add 150 g of the cheddar, the creamed sweetcorn, fresh sweetcorn, jalapeños, melted butter, eggs and ½ teaspoon salt and stir well. Taste and add more salt if necessary.

Pour the pudding into the baking pan and top with the remaining cheddar. Bake until just set, 45 to 50 minutes. Fire up the grill and grill until the top is browned, 1 to 2 minutes.

Sheet Pan CREAM & THYME ROASTED ONIONS

'Would this be good under a rib eye?' is a common question I ask myself when making sides. Just as common as me asking 'Would this be cute with cut-off Daisy Duke teen mum shorts?' as I online shop.

The answer to both is usually yes. But especially yes with this.

Spreading stuff out on baking sheets helps get it really golden and cooked really fast because it's more exposed to heat than when it's in a high-sided pan and crammed together. Sort of like lying on the beach without sunscreen or an umbrella (not that I know annnything about that, please erase my teenage years).

SERVES 4
ACTIVE TIME / 10 MIN
TOTAL TIME / 45 MIN

3 medium onions

5 sprigs fresh thyme, or 1 teaspoon dried

3 tablespoons olive oil

Kosher salt and freshly ground black pepper

60 ml double cream

Preheat the oven to 400°F/200°C. Line a rimmed baking sheet with foil.

Halve each onion vertically, then slice each half into 8 thin wedges. Put the onions in a large bowl and toss with the thyme, oil, and ½ teaspoon each salt and pepper. Dump the mixture on to the lined baking sheet, spread it out in one layer, and roast until the undersides are golden and a few edges are charred, 25 to 30 minutes.

Remove the onions from the oven, give them a stir, and season to taste with more salt and pepper. Drizzle the cream over the onions and return them to the oven to roast an additional 2 minutes or so, until the cream is bubbling and clings to the onions. Remove from the oven, discard the thyme sprigs, and season to taste with more salt and pepper.

Sweet & Savoury
HAM HOCK BAKED BEANS

It's not the sexiest thing to say, but baked beans have to be my absolute favourite BBQ side. I am verrrrry particular about them. They need to be bathing in a thick, syrupy bath and be slightly more sweet than tangy. But not too sweet. And just a little tangy. They need to be porky, but not so porky that it takes away from the soft, BUT NOT TOO SOFT, beauty beans.

And I know what you're thinking. FOUR hours for beans?? Yes. I'm sooooo sorry. I'm so sorry your house will smell like sweet, delicious beans and bacon for 3 hours and 45 minutes. How will you deal?! You poor thing. I'll pray for you!

SERVES 6 TO 8
ACTIVE TIME / 15 MIN
TOTAL TIME / 4 HRS

400 g dried haricot beans

6 slices bacon, cut into 2-cm pieces

1 medium onion, diced

4 cloves garlic, smashed

170 g tomato paste

1 tablespoon apple cider vinegar

2 teaspoons Worcestershire sauce

140 g dark brown sugar

1 tablespoon kosher salt, plus more to taste (see Tip)

2 teaspoons mustard powder, or 1 teaspoon English mustard

¼ teaspoon freshly ground black pepper

½ teaspoon cayenne pepper

1 ham hock, fresh or smoked

Preheat the oven to 300°F/150°C. Put the beans in a big oven-safe soup pot and cover them with water. Bring to a boil over high heat, reduce the heat and simmer for 25 minutes. Drain the beans and dry out the bottom of the pot.

Cook the bacon in the same pot over medium-high heat until rendered but not really crispy, about 3 minutes, and remove from the pot. Reduce the heat to medium, add the onion and garlic to the bacon grease and cook, stirring, until translucent, about 6 minutes. Add the tomato paste and cook, stirring, for 2 minutes. Add 1.25 litres water, the vinegar, Worcestershire, brown sugar, salt, mustard powder, pepper and cayenne.

Gently put the ham hock in the pot, return the bacon and beans to the pot, and bring it all to a boil over high heat. Cover and transfer the pot to the oven and cook until the beans are very tender and the meat falls off the bone, 2½ to 3 hours. Once an hour or so has passed, take a look in the pot and give it all a stir. If the water is getting below the level of the beans, add a little more just to cover.

When the beans and meat are done cooking, carefully remove the ham hock and, when it's just cool enough to handle, take all the meat off the bone and chop it up. Return the meat to the pot, taste, season with salt and pepper, and serve.

Tip / SEASONING WITH HOCKS

Ham hocks can vary in their saltiness, so you may need to add up to another tablespoon of salt to get the flavour right. Just taste after it's all been cooking for a while and then add salt to taste.

Sautéed SPICY ASPARAGUS

How spicy is this? Well Luna loves it so it isn't thaaaaat spicy. And for the record, asparagus doesn't make her OR my pee stink, so I don't know what all the fuss is about. Basically what I'm saying is we are beautiful, special unicorns. And if asparagus does make your pee stink and you can't handle it, or if you just want to eat another vegetable, this simple cooking method is great for so many things: green beans, spinach, Swiss chard, thin-cut carrots… it's all about stirring in that butter in the end.

SERVES 4
ACTIVE TIME / 10 MIN
TOTAL TIME / 15 MIN

1 bunch asparagus

2 tablespoons rapeseed or vegetable oil

½ teaspoon chilli flakes

¼ teaspoon smoked or regular paprika

Kosher salt and freshly ground black pepper

2 tablespoons butter

2 tablespoons chopped chives

Working with one at a time, hold an asparagus stalk horizontally and bend the tough bottom of the asparagus until it snaps off. Discard the snapped ends. Cut the asparagus into 5-cm lengths.

In a large frying pan, heat the oil over medium-high heat until very hot. Add the asparagus, chilli flakes, paprika, and salt and black pepper to taste. Cook, stirring, until tender-crisp, 2 to 3 minutes. Add the butter and toss to coat. Season again with salt and pepper and serve garnished with the chives.

Kung Pao
ROASTED BROCCOLI

I would kung pao anything if you gave me the chance. I'd eat things I normally wouldn't if they were kung pao'd. Innards? No. Kung pao innards? Sold. If you have somehow gotten to the part of your life where you are reading a recipe for kung pao'd something but have never actually eaten kung pao chicken from a Chinese takeout, it's a classic stir-fry with peanuts, chillies, garlic, vinegar, and a kind of pepper, Sichuan, that can be hard to find. So rather than have thousands of you tweet-assault me for recipes with unattainable ingredients, I left it out. Also, I don't *always* want meat (and, based on other tweet assaults, neither do you), so I decided to do this with little broccoli trees that absorb all of the spicy sweet savoury umami sauce that is Pao on the plate but Pow in your mouth.

SERVES 4
ACTIVE TIME / 15 MIN
TOTAL TIME / 40 MIN

FOR THE BROCCOLI

60 ml vegetable oil

1 tablespoon sesame oil

¼ teaspoon cayenne pepper, or more to taste

900 g broccoli (2 smallish heads), cut into florets, stems peeled and cut into 5-mm-thick rounds

Kosher salt and freshly ground black pepper

FOR THE KUNG PAO SAUCE

60 ml Thai sweet chilli sauce

2 tablespoons oyster sauce

2 tablespoons sesame oil

2 tablespoons vegetable oil

1½ tablespoons Sriracha

1 tablespoon soy sauce

1 tablespoon unseasoned rice vinegar

2 cloves garlic, finely minced

FOR GARNISH

40 g chopped salted roasted peanuts

1 spring onion, thinly sliced

1 fresh jalapeño (green or red), sliced into rings

ROAST THE BROCCOLI Preheat the oven to 400°F/200°C. In a bowl, whisk together the vegetable oil, sesame oil and cayenne. Toss the broccoli in the oil, then season generously with salt and pepper. Dump the broccoli on a large rimmed baking sheet, spread it out in one layer, and roast until the edges are blackened and crisp, 20 to 25 minutes.

MEANWHILE, MAKE THE SAUCE In a medium bowl, whisk together chilli sauce, oyster sauce, sesame oil, vegetable oil, Sriracha, soy sauce, vinegar and garlic.

Remove the broccoli from the oven and toss with the sauce directly on the pan. Turn the oven up to high or put the sheet under a hot grill and cook the broccoli until the sauce is thick and bubbling, 4 to 5 minutes. Transfer to a serving platter and garnish with the peanuts, spring onion and jalapeño.

Garlicky
CAULIFLOWER 'RICE'

Things-disguised-as-other-things usually annoy me, especially when it's for 'healthy' purposes but really is just an insult to your intelligence. This cauli rice passes the Chrissy Test, though, because it just tastes so f*cking good. (Note that I have a cauli mash in Book 1, so maybe cauliflower just has some spell over me where it can pretend to be a carb and I believe it.)

Anyway, to make cauliflower into 'rice', you *could* drag out the food processor, use it, and wash every last part, but aha! That plain old box grater you've previously used to shred mozzarella (and a knuckle or two) actually works great – I *prefer* the texture, as a matter of fact. Garlic, garlic, and more garlic jacks this up, but do with it what you will – cayenne, soy sauce – it's hard to ruin it!

SERVES 4 TO 6
ACTIVE TIME / 20 MIN
TOTAL TIME / 20 MIN

1 medium head cauliflower

60 ml olive oil

5 cloves garlic, minced

1 teaspoon kosher salt

¼ teaspoon freshly ground black pepper

Pinch of cayenne pepper

15 g chopped fresh basil, coriander, spring onions, parsley – whatever green stuff you want

Remove the leaves from the bottom of the cauliflower head. Cut the cauliflower in half and grate the cauliflower head on the large holes of a box grater until you reach the stem. (Or you can cut the florets off and pulse them in two batches in a food processer until it's ricey, about 30 seconds per batch.)

In a large frying pan, heat the oil over medium heat. Add the garlic and cook, stirring, until fragrant and light golden, 1 to 2 minutes. Add the cauliflower, salt, black pepper and cayenne and cook, stirring, until the 'rice' is tender, 6 to 7 minutes (a minute less for more al dente, a minute or two more for softer). Stir in the herbs and serve warm.

THAI
MOM

TOM YUM NOODLES

THIS IS ONE OF THE MOST IMPORTANT RECIPES IN MY LIFE. I am actually having trouble writing about it because I feel like there is such pressure to accurately convey how I feel about ONE OF THE MOST IMPORTANT RECIPES IN MY LIFE.

Tom yum is such a Thai classic and yet to anyone who hasn't made it before, such a mysterious little devil. Like, if its contents were a question on a game show, the only ingredient John would be sure of is water. And even then he would doubt himself and say but maybe it's chicken stock and then he would phone a friend and they'd be like, 'F*ck man, I dunno either.' Also why don't those friends ever just stand by with Google pulled up on their computers? Do they have someone watching them? Now I'm genuinely curious. I'm gonna phone a friend and ask.

Well, WONDER NO MORE! My mom has been making it this way my entire life. She knows my little quirks with it (I tend to not eat the prawns, leaving them in the bottom of the bowl with the lime leaf and lemongrass stalk, so she loads my bowl up with broth and shrooms) and I'm pretty sure the spice level of the bowl I ate on April 9, 2016, is single-handedly responsible for flipping Luna from breech to head-down in my uterus. What makes her tom yum special, you ask? Well, 1) you're a dick and 2) NOODLES. If you've ever been lucky enough to eat tom yum–flavoured Mama noodles (basically instant noodles, but made by Asians for Asians) then you knowwwwwwww how mind-numbingly awesome ramen would be in homemade soup. So we took the instant noodles, tossed out the seasoning packets, and boom. Tom yum noodle comfort food heaven.

SERVES 4 TO 6
ACTIVE TIME / 15 MIN*
TOTAL TIME / 45 MIN

2 chicken bouillon cubes

8 fresh Thai bird's eye chillies (these are hotttttt), or to taste

4 cloves garlic, halved

1 shallot, cut into 1-cm pieces

1 tablespoon fish sauce, plus more to taste

1 stalk fresh lemongrass (see Tip, page 99), cut into 5-cm pieces and lightly smashed

3 kaffir lime leaves, ** central vein removed**

2-cm piece fresh galangal (or ginger), cut into 5-mm-thick coins

1 (425-g) can straw mushrooms, drained and rinsed

12 cherry tomatoes, lightly smashed

2 (85-g) packets or 3 (65-g) packets instant ramen noodles***

4 spring onions, whites cut into 5-cm pieces, greens thinly sliced

450 g peeled and deveined king prawns

Kosher salt

Chopped fresh coriander, for garnish

Lime wedges, for serving

In a 4-litre saucepan, bring 2 litres water and the bouillon cubes to a boil. While the water is coming to a boil, place 5 of the chillies (or as many as you can handle) in a mortar with the garlic and shallot and mash until pulverized (or pulse them in a food processor, or chop together with a knife but, uh, don't touch your sensitive parts until after you've washed your hands one hundred times).

Add the chilli paste to the boiling liquid along with the fish sauce, lemongrass, kaffir lime leaves, galangal, mushrooms and tomatoes. Bring to a boil, reduce the heat, cover and simmer for 20 minutes to let the flavours infuse.

Uncover, add the noodles and spring onions, and simmer until the noodles are hydrated, about 2 minutes. Add the prawns and simmer until just cooked through, about 2 minutes. Season the soup to taste with salt or more fish sauce. Finely chop the remaining 3 chillies (or to taste, I'll say it again: They are hotttttt).

Discard the lime leaves and lemongrass stalks and divide the noodles and broth among bowls and garnish with the fresh chillies and coriander. Serve with lime wedges.

★

If you don't buy already cleaned prawns, this will be more like 30 minutes.

★★

Fresh (or frozen) kaffir lime leaves can sometimes be found at Asian markets; dried ones are almost always available in the Asian aisle or speciality stores, or use the internet.

★★★

Noodles only! Save the spice packets for another use.

PAD THAI CARBONARA (Bacon & Egg Pad Thai Spaghetti)

It is SO HARD to get a recipe out of my mom. She just . . . doesn't really have recipes. And she tends to use whatever's around. So one day, a signature dish of hers might have dark soy sauce, and the next day, light soy sauce with oyster sauce. It's maddening, but kind of amazing to see someone be able to adjust to absolutely anything.

I knew I had to have her pad Thai recipe in this book. But I could NOT for the life of me get her to make it the same way twice. Feeling defeated after a full day of noodling, I threw in the towel and hit the couch to watch the Emmy-worthy performances of the *Vanderpump Rules* cast.

Then, one morning, I heard a bag of noodles open in the kitchen behind me. Then I smelled bacon.

She was making *bacon pad Thai*. Out of nowhere. And I missed it.

I made her do it again when it was fresh in her head with the only noodles we had left – spaghetti. OH, IT WAS A DELIGHT. The entire world stopped. I posted it on Twitter and was flooded with inquiries. Some asked what time to come over. Some offered to send an Uber for pad Thai pickup. Some asked why the f*ck we were making spaghetti at 8:45 a.m.

Eggs and bacon make it a whole lot like a carbonara, but the Thai flavours make it pad Thai. You are so very welcome for this beautiful hybrid beast.

SERVES 4
ACTIVE TIME / 10 MIN
TOTAL TIME / 25 MIN

1 small head broccoli

2½ tablespoons sweet soy sauce*

1 tablespoon liquid soybean paste**

1½ teaspoons fish sauce, plus more to taste

1½ teaspoons low-sodium soy sauce, plus more to taste

3 slices thick-cut bacon, cut into 2-cm squares

4 cloves garlic, roughly chopped

½ teaspoon Thai chilli powder (see page 153), or to taste

125 ml chicken stock, plus more if needed

225 g spaghetti, cooked to al dente, drained, and oiled

2 eggs, beaten

2 spring onions, cut into 2-cm lengths

Separate the broccoli crown from the stem. Trim the end off the stem, peel it, and cut it crosswise into 5-mm-thick coins. Separate the crown into small florets.

In a small bowl, whisk together the sweet soy, soybean paste, fish sauce, and soy sauce. This is your sauce.

In a wok or very large sauté pan, cook the bacon over medium heat until just gently crisped (I mean, don't go crazy; just get most of the fat rendered), 6 to 7 minutes. Add the garlic and chilli powder and cook, stirring, for 1 minute. Increase the heat to medium-high, add the sauce, and cook until reduced slightly, about 1 minute. Add the broccoli, splash with half the chicken stock, and cook until just tender, 3 to 5 minutes. Increase the heat to high. Add the spaghetti and the rest of the stock and cook, tossing, until very hot and the sauce is absorbed, 3 to 5 minutes (if it feels too dry, splash in more stock or water a little at a time). Season with additional soy sauce and fish sauce to taste.

Remove the pan from the heat, add the eggs, and toss until the eggs are creamy. Toss in the spring onions and serve.

★   This is liquid gold: It's soy sauce thickened with palm sugar molasses and it tastes caramely and salty and like heaven, basically. Look for Thai brands like Healthy Boy or the Indonesian version, which is called *kecap manis*.

★★   This is a chunky Thai sauce that's like a cross between miso and fermented Chinese black beans, with a little sweetness. If you can't find it, you can buy a jar of fermented Chinese black beans, fish out some of it, and combine it with an equal amount of light brown sugar.

Pork GLASS NOODLE SALAD

This garlicky-tart-savoury 'salad' of ground pork and noodles is also known as *yum woon sen*. I love my Thai people. I love a language that puts 'yum' in the *name* of its food. Like when a company calls itself #1 Nail Salon or The Country's Best Yogurt. Or like if I called this book *Oprah's Book Club #1 Choice Cravings*. Or like if a young R&B artist decided his last name should be 'Legend'. Sometimes, you just gotta name it and claim it. These noodles are Yum-my. I dare you to disagree.

90 g dried glass noodles (a.k.a. bean thread or cellophane noodles)

4 cloves garlic

2 fresh Thai birds eye chillies, or to taste, plus slices for garnish

1 small clove Thai pickled garlic, plus 1 tablespoon of the pickle juice (see Note)

3 tablespoons fish sauce

2 tablespoons fresh lime juice (from 1 lime), plus lime wedges for serving

450 g ground pork

1 teaspoon kosher salt

1 large tomato, cut into 10 wedges

½ small white onion, cut into thin half-moons

3 spring onions, cut into 3-cm lengths

20 g tender celery leaves (literally the leaves that come with your celery stalks)

20 g shredded mint leaves

Place the noodles in a medium bowl and cover with cold water; let them soak until they hydrate, about 15 minutes. While the noodles are soaking, fill a large saucepan halfway with water and bring to a boil over high heat.

Drop the hydrated noodles into the boiling water for 2 minutes. Drain in a colander and let cool slightly.

With a mortar and pestle, mash the garlic, chillies (they're hot!), and pickled garlic (or chop it all finely with a knife) until pulverized. Transfer to a small bowl and whisk in the pickled garlic juice, fish sauce and lime juice with a fork.

Heat a large frying pan over medium-high heat. Add the pork and salt and cook, breaking up the meat into tiny pieces with a wooden spoon, until browned and cooked through, 5 to 6 minutes. Cool slightly.

In a large bowl, combine the pork, drained noodles, tomato, onion, spring onions, celery leaves and mint. Add the garlic-lime dressing and toss. Divide among bowls, garnish with thinly sliced chillies, and serve with lime wedges.

Note / *THAI PICKLED GARLIC*

Thai pickled garlic is available at Asian markets. If you can't find it, use 1 small clove garlic and 2 teaspoons unseasoned rice vinegar or distilled white vinegar and 1 teaspoon sugar in place of the pickle juice.

KHAO TOD
(Crispy Rice Salad) with Fried Eggs

This salad has lots of wonderful ingredients, like peanuts, ginger and herbs, but the headliner is the crisped-up rice. Some people make it with rice balls, but I like to make the rice cakes thinner to give the rice more surface area, which means maximum crispiness. Oh, and we top it with a sunny-side-up egg, which makes everything better. (This trick works with a pizza, a burger, meatballs, asparagus . . . yeah, pretty much everything.)

SERVES 4
ACTIVE TIME / 20 MIN
TOTAL TIME / 40 MIN

1 litre peanut oil, for frying

60 g plus 1 tablespoon plain flour

5 eggs

2 teaspoons red chilli paste or sambal oelek

750 g cooked jasmine rice, cooled if you made it fresh for this*

4 dried chillies (such as árbol), or to taste

35 g peanuts

3 tablespoons fresh lime juice (from about 1½ limes)

1 tablespoon fish sauce or soy sauce

2 teaspoons sugar

1 teaspoon Thai chilli powder (see Tip), or to taste

10 g loosely packed fresh coriander leaves

10 g loosely packed mint leaves

20 g sliced spring onions

2 shallots, sliced into very thin wedges

2-cm piece fresh ginger, peeled and cut into thin matchsticks (julienne)

★ If you're making fresh rice for this recipe, DON'T rinse the rice before cooking; the starch is your friend and will help the rice cakes stick together.

In a 23-cm cast-iron frying pan, heat the oil over medium-high heat to 350°F/180°C. (Use a deep-fry thermometer or test the oil by dropping in a grain of rice; if it sizzles immediately but isn't burning, you're good.)

While the oil is heating, make the rice cakes: Put the flour in a shallow dish. In a large bowl, whisk together 1 egg, the chilli paste and the remaining 1 tablespoon flour. Add the rice and mix with your hands. Form the mixture into 8 patties 7.5 cm wide and 3 cm thick. Dredge the patties in the flour and set on a plate.

Fry the dried chillies and peanuts in the oil just enough to darken them slightly, being careful not to burn them, 1 to 2 minutes. Remove with a slotted spoon and drain on paper towels; set aside for garnish.

Working in two batches, use a Chinese spider or slotted spoon to gently lower the rice cakes into the oil and fry them until crispy and golden brown, flipping halfway, about 5 minutes per side. Remove the cakes from the oil and allow them to cool on paper towels.

In a small bowl, whisk together the lime juice, fish sauce, sugar and chilli powder until the sugar is dissolved.

Using your hands, crumble up the crispy rice cakes into different sizes into a bowl. Add the coriander, mint, spring onions, shallots and ginger.

Take a bit of the frying oil and heat it up in a separate frying pan, then fry 4 eggs sunny-side-up style.

Toss the salad with the dressing, divide the salad among four plates, and top each plate with a sunny-side-up egg. Garnish with the fried peanuts and chillies.

Tip / *HOMEMADE THAI CHILLI POWDER*

Buy dried Thai chillies (available at Thai markets) or dried serrano or árbol chillies (available at Mexican markets) and grind them up in a spice grinder or with a mortar and pestle until fine. It lasts indefinitely in a sealed container at room temp.

Thai **FISHCAKES**
with Spicy Peanut Sauce

I think we can all agree that some things were birthed strictly as sauce vessels. I like steak, but I really eat it for the A.1. Is that wrong? Sometimes a sauce is just *that* good – this is one of them. The pan-fried fishcakes are flavourful little buggers, with a ton of fresh herbs and a nice pop of crunch from the green beans, but the sauce is the dip of little spicy sweet coconut peanut angels.

SERVES 4
ACTIVE TIME / 30 MIN
TOTAL TIME / 30 MIN

FOR THE SPICY PEANUT SAUCE

85 ml full-fat coconut milk, shaken

120 g chunky peanut butter

1 teaspoon finely grated lime zest

Juice of 2 medium limes

2 teaspoons soy sauce

2 teaspoons fish sauce

2 teaspoons finely minced fresh hot chilli, or to taste

5 teaspoons light brown sugar

FOR THE FISHCAKES

450 g skinless fish fillet, such as snapper or cod, cut into large chunks

Finely grated zest of ½ lime

1 tablespoon Thai red curry paste (buy it)

1 teaspoon kosher salt

25 g fresh coriander leaves

25 g fresh basil leaves

3 cloves garlic, minced

2 small shallots, chopped

½ small jalapeño

1 egg

6 tablespoons cornflour

6 green beans, trimmed and very thinly sliced crosswise into circles

Vegetable oil, for shallow-frying

Fresh coriander leaves, for garnish

MAKE THE SPICY PEANUT SAUCE In a small saucepan, combine the coconut milk, peanut butter, lime zest, lime juice, soy sauce, fish sauce, chilli, and brown sugar. Melt, stirring, over medium heat. Remove from the heat, transfer to a serving bowl, and let cool.

MAKE THE FISHCAKES In a food processor, combine the fish, lime zest, curry paste, salt, coriander, basil, garlic, shallots, jalapeño, egg and cornflour and pulse until everything is very finely minced but not *totalllllly* pasty, 20 to 25 pulses. Open the processor, sprinkle in the green beans, and pulse 5 more times to mix in evenly.

Using wet hands, form 3 to 4 tablespoons of the fishcake mixture into a ball and flatten it to about 5-mm thickness. Form the rest of the cakes this way.

In a large frying pan, heat 5 mm vegetable oil over medium-high heat until shimmering-hot but not smoking. Working in batches, arrange as many cakes as you can fit comfortably in the pan and fry until golden, 2 to 3 minutes per side. Drain on paper towels. Serve the fishcakes with the sauce and garnish with coriander.

Crab **FRIED RICE**

LADIES AND GENTLEMEN, INTRODUCING MY MOM, PEPPER THAI!!: 'For seafood lovers. I like crabmeat. It's very expensive, but at the end of the month, when Daddy got paid, we got crabmeat. And we fried rice. And we loved it! It's the best fried rice. Sometimes I drove all the way to the beach (two hours!) to get crabmeat. When Chrissy was young, I went crabbing. I prefer Dungeness crab, but canned crab is fine, too.'

SERVES 4
ACTIVE TIME / 10 MIN
TOTAL TIME / 55 MIN

- 350 g raw jasmine rice, or 720 g cups leftover cooked rice
- 60 ml peanut or vegetable oil
- 1 large onion, sliced
- 2 spring onions, cut into 2-cm lengths, plus thinly sliced spring onion greens for garnish
- 6 cloves garlic, minced
- 3 eggs, lightly beaten
- 60 ml soy sauce
- 1 large beef tomato, seeded (see Tip) and cut into wedges
- 225 g white crabmeat, drained
- Kosher salt and ground white pepper
- Chilli Oil (recipe follows), for drizzling
- Fresh coriander, for garnish

Cook the rice 2 minutes less than the package directions so it is al dente. Spread the rice on a baking sheet to cool quickly and prevent it from overcooking and getting mushy. (If you're using cold leftover rice, put it in a bowl or on a rimmed baking sheet and break it up so it's not in huge clumps.)

In a large wok or very large sauté pan, heat the oil over medium-high heat until shimmering but not smoking. Add the onion and cook until just soft, 3 to 4 minutes. Add the spring onions and garlic and cook, stirring, for 1 minute. Add the eggs, letting them sit and cook for 20 seconds until partially set, and add the rice and then the soy sauce, mixing everything together and breaking up the eggs as you do. Cook, stirring, until the rice is hot. Add the tomato and crab and cook until warmed through, 1 to 2 minutes. Season to taste with salt and white pepper. Drizzle with chilli oil to taste and garnish with spring onion greens and coriander.

Tip / *HOW TO SEED A TOMATO*

Quarter the tomato through the core and use your fingers to scoop out all the jelly-like liquid and seeds between the tomato's inner walls. Eat it like candy or reserve for another use.

Chilli Oil

250 ml vegetable oil

2 heaped tablespoons chilli flakes

In a small saucepan, warm the oil over medium-high heat until a pepper flake sizzles slightly when you drop it in the oil. Add the chilli flakes and cook over the lowest heat possible until fragrant, 3 to 4 minutes. Remove from the heat and cool. The oil will get spicier the longer it infuses. Store, refrigerated in an airtight container, for up to 1 month.

MAKES 250 ML
ACTIVE TIME / 1 MIN
TOTAL TIME / 5 MIN

Pork **LARB**

It's crunchy, spicy, sour and meaty. But it has vegetables around it, so let's call this pile of sautéed, dressed pork a salad. I love putting pork larb in a little cabbage-leaf boat. It's kinda like a P.F. Chang's lettuce wrap, but Thai. We'll call it P.F. Changaporn's (almost every Thai last name ends in 'porn'). OK, it's not as funny if you have to explain it. But this is still the sexiest salad ever!

SERVES 4
ACTIVE TIME / 15 MIN
TOTAL TIME / 20 MIN

2 tablespoons peanut oil

450 g ground pork

Kosher salt

1 tablespoon Toasted Rice Powder (recipe follows)

¼ teaspoon toasted Thai red chilli powder (see Tip), or ½ teaspoon chilli flakes

2 tablespoons fresh lime juice (from 1 lime), plus 4 lime wedges for serving

2 tablespoons fish sauce

100 g thinly sliced red onion

1 spring onion, thinly sliced

1 tablespoon chopped fresh coriander

1 tablespoon chopped fresh mint

Ground white pepper

350 g shredded green cabbage or whole small cabbage leaves, for serving

Cooked white rice, for serving

In a large heavy frying pan, heat the oil over medium-high heat. Add the pork and ¼ teaspoon salt and cook, breaking up the meat into tiny pieces with a wooden spoon, until cooked through, 4 to 5 minutes. (Don't worry about browning the meat; just get it cooked.) Transfer the meat to a bowl.

In a separate bowl, whisk the toasted rice powder, chilli powder, lime juice and fish sauce. Add the sauce to the pork. Toss in the onion, spring onion, coriander and mint. Season to taste with salt and white pepper. Serve with lime wedges, cabbage and rice.

Tip / *TOASTED THAI RED CHILLI POWDER*

Super spicy and warm, you can buy this at Thai stores or make it yourself by toasting any amount of dried Thai bird's eye chillies (or a combo of Thai birds eye and other dried hot red chillies) in a dry pan over medium-high heat until they get brittle and crisp, 3 to 4 minutes. Cool and process in a spice grinder or mash up with a mortar and pestle.

Toasted Rice Powder

100 g jasmine rice

In a dry frying pan, toast the rice over medium heat
until browned, shaking the pan often to prevent
burning, 12 to 14 minutes. Transfer the rice to a plate to
cool completely. Pound with a mortar and pestle until
as fine as fine breadcrumbs (you can also do this in a
spice grinder or a completely dry blender). Stored in an
airtight container, it keeps forever.

MAKES ABOUT 100 G
ACTIVE TIME / 15 MIN
TOTAL TIME / 15 MIN

Thai SEARED TUNA SALAD

After Luna was born, it was tough adjusting to life as a new mom. I've been open about my postpartum depression. It was great to finally admit it and work on getting better. Part of me getting better was going away with my family on a two-week wellness retreat in Bali. We didn't drink, we ate healthy foods, we did Pilates every day. It was so the opposite of how I normally live. And I LOVED it.

During our stay in Bali, we took some amazing cooking classes and I fell in love with so many new flavours. Healthy flavours. Bright flavours. Even the ones that weren't new felt like it, since I could focus on how clean and light they felt. Like in this flaked tuna salad with lime juice and chillies and herbs. It's spicy and sour and will make you feel like you're in the middle of the Balinese jungle being healthy and sh*t.

SERVES 4
ACTIVE TIME / 25 MIN
TOTAL TIME / 30 MIN
(or 90 minutes with marinating time)

FOR THE SALAD

450 g tuna steak, brought to room temp for 20 to 30 minutes

Extra-virgin olive oil

Kosher salt and freshly ground black pepper

50 g chopped seeded cucumber

75 g 5-cm lengths green beans

100 g halved cherry tomatoes

35 g thinly sliced shallots

15 g chopped fresh mint

15 g chopped fresh coriander

FOR THE DRESSING

1 to 2 fresh Thai birds eye chillies (hot!!), or ¼ jalapeño if you want it a little milder

3 large cloves garlic

2 tablespoons fish sauce

2 tablespoons fresh lime juice

PREPARE THE SALAD Lightly coat the tuna with olive oil on both sides and season generously with salt and pepper. Heat a dry heavy frying pan over high heat until very hot but not smoking. Sear the tuna until browned but still rare in the middle, turning once, 2 minutes per side. Transfer the tuna to a cutting board and let rest for 5 minutes. Using two forks, flake the tuna into large chunks and put them in a bowl. Add the cukes, green beans, tomatoes, shallots, some of the mint and some of the coriander and toss together.

MAKE THE DRESSING With a mortar and pestle or with the side of a knife, mash the chillies and garlic together. Transfer to a bowl and whisk together with the fish sauce and lime juice.

Add the dressing to the tuna mixture. You can serve the salad right away, but it's better if you let it marinate, tossing occasionally, for 1 hour. Serve with the remaining mint and coriander on top.

Red CHICKEN CURRY

If you learn to keep a can or jar of red curry paste in the house (most supermarkets have it these days), you're well on your way to this Pepper Thai creation, which basically came together one night while I was on the couch in a towel deciding which Snapchat filter to use to obscure my actual face. When Mom fishes through her Special Thai Drawer in the fridge (enter at your own risk), she decides on a dinner dish before you've even decided you're hungry . . . which you def will be once you smell the ginger and garlic and fish sauce and brown sugar and you get a look at those juicy thighs braising with broccoli and peppers and onions all up in the spicy, sweet coconutty sauce.

SERVES 4
ACTIVE TIME / 20 MIN
TOTAL TIME / 1 HR

- 8 boneless, skinless chicken thighs, patted dry
- Kosher salt and freshly ground black pepper
- 2 tablespoons rapeseed oil
- 1 small onion, sliced
- 2 tablespoons finely minced fresh ginger
- 6 cloves garlic, finely minced
- 2 tablespoons Thai red curry paste (buy that sh*t)
- 1 (400 ml) can full-fat coconut milk, shaken
- 2 tablespoons light brown sugar
- 1 tablespoon fish sauce, or more to taste

- 1 large red pepper, cored, seeded, and sliced
- 1 large yellow pepper, cored, seeded, and sliced
- 1 medium potato, peeled and cut into 2-cm chunks
- 350 g broccoli florets (cut larger florets in half to make them bite-size)
- ¼ teaspoon ground white pepper
- 1 teaspoon chopped jalapeño, plus more for garnish
- Cooked jasmine rice, for serving
- Chopped fresh basil, for garnish

Season the chicken generously with salt and pepper. In a large heavy-bottomed pot or casserole dish, heat the oil over medium-high heat. Brown the chicken all at once (it's OK if they don't all lie flat in the pot; we're saving time here) until golden, 4 to 5 minutes per side. Transfer the chicken to a plate.

Add the onion to the pot and cook, stirring, until just softened, about 4 minutes. Add the ginger, garlic and curry paste and cook, stirring, until fragrant, about 2 minutes. Stir in the coconut milk, brown sugar and fish sauce until smooth. Bring to a boil, reduce the heat to medium-low, and simmer about 2 minutes. Stir in the peppers and potato, then return the chicken with any juices to the pot. Cover and simmer until the chicken and potatoes are just cooked through, about 20 minutes.

While the curry is cooking, place the broccoli and 1 cm of water in a microwave-safe bowl. Cover and microwave on high until the broccoli turns bright green, about 3 minutes. Drain.

Uncover the curry and stir in the broccoli, ½ teaspoon salt (or more to taste), white pepper and jalapeño and simmer, uncovered, until the liquid thickens slightly, about 3 minutes. Serve with rice and garnish with basil and more jalapeño.

Thai SOY-GARLIC FRIED RIBS

Making ribs at home can be sooooo intimidating. Pretty much every rib recipe involves hours of smoking or slow-baking and, in the end, I'm saying, 'I could have just ordered these from Uncle Andre's.' (That's one of our favourite L.A. BBQ spots. #nospon #notpaidforthat.) Anyway, enter Pepper Thai with the perfect solution: Fry the ribs! These Thai fried ribs are so easy! Just a few ingredients and a few minutes and you have hot, juicy ribs with a soy-garlic-rubbed Thai twist. Fry some ribs for your next football party. Your friends will leave happy even if the other team scores all the home runs.

SERVES 2 TO 4
ACTIVE TIME / 10 MIN
TOTAL TIME / 25 MIN

1 rack baby back pork ribs (12 to 14 ribs), separated into individual ribs

2 tablespoons soy sauce

7 cloves garlic, finely minced

1 teaspoon freshly ground black pepper

2 litres vegetable oil, for deep-frying

Pepper's Red-Hot Pepper Sauce (recipe follows), for serving

Put the ribs in a large bowl. Add the soy sauce, garlic and pepper and toss to coat. Let stand at room temperature.

Heat the oil in a large heavy pot over medium-high heat to 370°F/190°C. (Use a deep-fry thermometer or test the oil by throwing in a little piece of bread or some bread crumbs; if they sizzle immediately but aren't burning, you're ready.) Working in batches of 4 or 5, fry the ribs until just cooked and well browned, 3 to 4 minutes. Bring the oil back to 370°F/190°C between batches and try to skim out any stray bits of garlic so they don't burn in the oil and make it taste like burnt garlic.

Serve with Pepper's red-hot pepper sauce or just watch your baby chew on them with nothing at all!

Pepper's Red-Hot Pepper Sauce

Yes, this was in my first book. It didn't stop being delicious.

2 tablespoons toasted Thai red chilli powder (see Tip, page 161)

2 tablespoons hot water

2 tablespoons fish sauce

1 tablespoon Toasted Rice Powder (page 163)

10 baby plum or cherry tomatoes, halved

In a small bowl, combine the chilli powder and hot water. Stir in the fish sauce and toasted rice powder. Squeeze in the pulp of the tomatoes (discard the skins) and stir together. The sauce will keep in the fridge for a week or so.

MAKES 125 ML
ACTIVE TIME / 5 MIN
TOTAL TIME / 5 MIN

Pepper's
SPRING ROLLS

Asian cuisines have given us an efficient way to get all the food groups into one cute little package: the spring roll! Actually, I don't even know what the food groups are any more. Are they a pyramid? Did Michelle Obama change it and then did Melania plagiarize it as her own? I don't know. Anyway, my mom's spring rolls are sure to bring together both sides of the aisle. They're crispy on the outside, juicy and savoury on the inside. They're fried. And they have vegetables, too!

MAKES 20 TO 25
SPRING ROLLS
ACTIVE TIME / 30 MIN
TOTAL TIME / 1 HR

450 g ground pork

225 g prawns, peeled, deveined, and finely minced

200 g soft tofu, drained of most of its liquid

300 g bean sprouts

225 g finely chopped celery

1 small onion, finely chopped

3 cloves garlic, minced

1 tablespoon soy sauce

1 tablespoon kosher salt

1 teaspoon freshly ground black pepper

2 egg whites

8 cups rapeseed or vegetable oil, for deep-frying

1 package large (20-cm) spring roll wrappers*

Thai sweet chilli sauce or hoisin sauce, for serving

In a bowl, use your hands to mash up the pork, prawns, tofu, bean sprouts, celery, onion, garlic, soy sauce, salt and pepper until well incorporated. Place the egg whites in a bowl.

Pour the oil into a 4- to 5-litre saucepan over medium heat and heat to 370°F/190°C. (Use a deep-fry thermometer or test the oil by throwing in a little piece of bread or some bread crumbs; if they sizzle immediately but aren't burning, you're ready. If the oil comes to temperature before you're ready to start frying, turn the heat down to low to maintain the temperature and then turn it back up to medium when you're about ready to cook.)

Meanwhile, lay out a spring roll wrapper on a work surface and moisten the edges with egg white. Spread around 100 g of the filling mixture in a stripe one-third of the way up from the bottom of the wrapper, leaving a 2-cm border on each side. Lift the wrapper up from the bottom over the filling, roll a bit, then fold in the sides and continue to wrap until tightly sealed into a log, brushing the final seam with egg white to seal. Continue making spring rolls until all of the filling and/or wrappers are used up.

When the oil is at the right temperature, working in batches of 4 or 5 at a time (and letting the oil come back to temperature between batches), fry the spring rolls until golden brown, about 5 minutes. Drain the spring rolls on paper towels. Serve with sweet chilli sauce or hoisin sauce.

★ Usually you'll see two sizes of wrappers in the refrigerator section, weirdly often in the fruit and veg aisle; get the larger ones. The number of wrappers in a package can vary from anywhere between 20 and 25. If you come up short on filling, you can use the leftover wrappers for the Lazy Prawn & Pork 'Wonton' Soup (page 44). If you end up with a little extra filling, you can always stir-fry it, season it to taste, and serve it over rice.

THAI MOM **173**

SUPPER

SCALLOP LINGUINE
with Casino Bread Crumbs

So for this recipe I wrote a whole thing about how much I freaking love New Orleans for its baked oysters and regrettable yardstick drinks and Clams Casino, but then my editor told me that Clams Casino are from Rhode Island, so I had to scrap it. Anyway, Clams Casino – baked clams with cheese and bread crumbs and bacon – are heaven. But scallops are better than clams and pasta is better than not-pasta, so here.

SERVES 4
ACTIVE TIME / 35 MIN
TOTAL TIME / 35 MIN

FOR THE CASINO BREAD CRUMBS

- **4 slices white bread, torn into pieces, or 180 g panko bread crumbs, but fresh is better! (see Tip, page 178)**
- **3 slices bacon, chopped crosswise**
- **1 tablespoon butter**
- **3 cloves garlic, finely minced**
- **½ teaspoon kosher salt**
- **½ teaspoon freshly ground black pepper**
- **20 g finely grated Parmigiano-Reggiano cheese**

FOR THE PASTA AND SCALLOPS

- **Kosher salt**
- **300 g linguine**
- **340 g scallops (12 large, or more if they're smaller)**
- **Canola oil, for searing**
- **Freshly ground black pepper**
- **125 ml chicken stock**
- **2 tablespoons butter**
- **185 ml sour cream**
- **40 g finely grated Parmigiano-Reggiano or Pecorino Romano cheese, or more to taste**
- **35 g finely chopped chives, plus more for garnish**

MAKE THE BREAD CRUMBS In a food processor, process the bread until it forms fine crumbs, then dump them into a bowl. (If you're using panko, skip the food processor and just put the panko in a bowl.)

In a large frying pan, cook the bacon over medium-low heat, stirring occasionally, until rendered and crisp, about 5 minutes. Remove the bacon bits from the pan but leave the fat in there. Add the butter, swish to melt, then add the garlic and cook, stirring, until the garlic smells great but hasn't browned, 1 to 2 minutes. Add the bread crumbs, increase the heat to medium, and brown the crumbs, stirring frequently, until toasty, 7 to 8 minutes (or a couple of minutes less if using panko). Stir in the salt and pepper, remove from the heat, and transfer to a large plate to cool for 5 minutes. Crumble the bacon until fine, then toss it into the bread crumbs along with the Parm.

MAKE THE PASTA AND SCALLOPS Bring a large pot of salted water (I mean, salt it enough so that the water tastes good. Not 'salty like the sea', because who the hell likes drinking seawater?) to a boil. Cook the pasta according to the package directions. (Or, if you're paranoid like me about overcooking pasta, wait a few minutes to start cooking it until the scallops are in the pan.)

CONTINUES

Pat the scallops dry with paper towels. Don't salt them yet (it makes the tops wet so just hold your horses!). Heat a large frying pan (NOT nonstick) over medium-high heat for 2 minutes. It should be really hot but not screaming hot. Add enough oil to slick the bottom of the pan. Season the scallops generously with salt and pepper and add them to the pan, seasoned-side down. DO NOT MOVE THEM! DO NOT TOUCH THEM! THIS IS THE ULTIMATE DFWI MOMENT. YOU WILL THANK ME!

Cook the scallops until a crust forms, 1½ to 2 minutes. Now this is gonna sound crazy, but just go with me here: Carefully pat the tops of the scallops down with a paper towel while they're cooking, season the top sides with salt and pepper, and flip the scallops. Cook for another minute, 1½ minutes max. (Cook them for less time on both sides if you're using small scallops.) Move the scallops to a plate, and wipe out the pan if it is too dark, otherwise just add the stock to the pan and stir to scrape up any browned bits, then cook until the liquid is reduced by half. (It'll be quick.) Whisk in the butter. Add the sour cream and salt and pepper to taste. Whisk until smooth and cook until hot, maybe 1 minute. Remove from the heat.

When the pasta is ready, drain it, keeping a little bit of the pasta water. Add the pasta to the sour cream mixture and toss to coat. If it looks dry, splash in a little pasta water. Return the scallops and any juices to the pasta, then add the Parm, half the bread crumbs and the chives and toss. Divide among bowls and top with the remaining bread crumbs and more chives.

Tip / *HOW TO MAKE FAST FRESH BREAD CRUMBS*

Any time you need bread crumbs but don't have any in the house, making fresh bread crumbs out of bread – which you probably *do* have lying around – takes only a couple seconds and saves you a trip to the store. (Or, uh, asking people on the Internet to give you some.) It's really as simple as the first step in this recipe.

SLEEPYTIME STEW & Cream Cheese Smashed Potatoes

I cannot say this enough: I LOVE STEW. I love everything about it. I love a thick, deeply flavourful, beefy broth. Giant chunks of potatoes. Sweet carrots poking up through tender hunks of chuck.

I first made this on a rainy day in upstate New York. We had wanted to get out of the city for a bit, so we packed the dogs into a Hertz and away we went. 'This is some f*ckin stew weather,' I said. But ALAS! I had no recipe and only a history of Dinty Moore. I did my best and spooned the specimen on to a hearty dollop of red smashed potatoes. IT WAS HEAVEN. Not perfect (I overcooked my beef by browning it too long), but oh, the flavour. I made it a couple more times that week and slapped the recipe on to my blog and the comments and tweets flooded in. There was so much love for my sleepytime stew!

It took a while to perfect, but there isn't a rainy Sunday that passes without me making this exact recipe, right here.

Why the 'sleepytime'? You'll see.

SERVES 8 TO 10
ACTIVE TIME / 40 MIN
TOTAL TIME / 3 HRS 30 MIN

FOR THE STEW

5 tablespoons olive oil

2 tablespoons butter

900 g beef stew meat (rump steak), cut into 5-cm chunks

Kosher salt and freshly ground black pepper

1 medium onion, cut into 2-cm dice

4 cloves garlic, minced

60 g tomato paste

1 litre beef stock, plus more as needed

1 teaspoon Worcestershire sauce

½ teaspoon sugar

2 large or 6 small carrots, cut into 5-cm chunks

2 celery stalks, cut into 5-cm chunks

1 (425-g) can white beans, drained and rinsed

1 jalapeño, chopped (keep the seeds in if you can handle the spice – optional, but *do it*)

2 bay leaves

FOR THE POTATOES

1.25 kg potatoes, skin-on, halved

Kosher salt

8 tablespoons butter, cut into chunks, at room temperature

225 g cream cheese, cut into chunks, at room temperature

125 ml double cream, at room temperature

1 teaspoon seasoned salt, or to taste

2 cloves roasted garlic (if you have some lying around. I do, because I am like that), smashed (see page 107)

CONTINUES

MAKE THE STEW In a large heavy-bottomed pot, heat half the oil and butter over medium-high heat. Pat the meat dry with paper towels. Season half the meat well with salt and pepper, add to the pot, and sear without touching for 3 minutes. Then turn the pieces every few minutes, searing all over, until deeply browned on all sides, about 12 minutes total per batch. Move this first batch to a plate. If the pot is really dark after the first batch, splash in some water, scrape up the browned bits, and keep that with the seared meat. Wipe out the pot and continue with the remaining oil, butter and meat (seasoning it first).

Transfer the second batch of meat to the plate with the first batch of meat. Discard all but 3 tablespoons of the fat from the pot. Add the onion and garlic to the pot and cook, making sure to scrape up any last browned bits and stains from the bottom with a wooden spoon (flavour!), 6 to 7 minutes. Add the tomato paste, again, scraping those browned bits, and cook until the tomato paste is a little rust coloured, about 2 minutes.

Add the beef stock to the pot, scraping those last bits of brown up from the bottom of the pot one more time, then add the Worcestershire and sugar. Return the seared beef and any juices from the plate to the pot, bring to a boil, reduce the heat to a bare simmer, cover, and simmer over medium-low heat until the liquid thickens and darkens, about 2 hours.

Throw in the carrots, celery, white beans, jalapeño and bay leaves. Cover and let simmer for another hour (if you can wait that long!). Season to taste with salt and pepper.

ABOUT 45 MINUTES BEFORE THE STEW IS DONE, MAKE THE POTATOES In a large pot, combine the potatoes with water to cover by 5 cm. Salt it well, bring to a boil, reduce the heat, and simmer until the potatoes are cooked, about 25 minutes. Drain well, return to the pot, and smash with one of those potato masher things until chunky. Stir in the butter, cream cheese and double cream. Add the seasoned salt and smashed roasted garlic (if using).

Serve the stew with the potatoes. Dunzo!

CHEDDAR-CHORIZO BROCCOLI RICE
in Tomato Bowls

When you love cheddar-broccoli soup like I do, you will bring its flavours to as many meals as possible. So you fill a juicy tomato 'bowl' with cheesy, broccoli-studded rice, bake to bubbly perfection, and think you've got them nailed. But then you become eight months pregnant and you realize hours before your cookbook is about to print that this dish would be *oh, so much better* with sausage. So you essentially STOP THE PRESSES, and rework the recipe to include chorizo. Then, and only then, is your cookbook complete.

SERVES 4
ACTIVE TIME / 25 MIN
TOTAL TIME / 50 MIN

4 extra-large firm-ripe beef tomatoes (350 g each*)

1 tablespoon vegetable oil

225 g fresh chorizo sausage, casings removed

Kosher salt and freshly ground black pepper

1 tablespoon plain flour

250 ml whole milk

100 g grated extra-mature cheddar cheese

40 g finely grated Parmigiano-Reggiano cheese

¼ teaspoon cayenne pepper, or to taste

280 g cooked rice

210 g broccoli florets, chopped into little bits

45 g seasoned dried bread crumbs

In a large frying pan, heat the oil over medium-high heat. Add the chorizo, season lightly with salt and pepper, and cook, breaking up with a spoon, until the fat is rendered and the chorizo is golden, 6 to 7 minutes. Transfer the chorizo and the rendered fat into a bowl. (You should have about 3 tablespoons of fat.) Return 1 tablespoon of the fat to the pan, add the flour, and cook, stirring, until it turns dirty blond in colour and smells a little nutty, 2 to 3 minutes.

Whisk in the milk, bring to a boil, reduce the heat to medium, and cook, whisking, until it thickens, 2 to 3 minutes. Add the cheddar, parm, cayenne, 1 teaspoon salt, and ¼ teaspoon black pepper and whisk the sauce until smooth. Add the rice, broccoli and cooked chorizo and season with more salt, black pepper, and cayenne to taste.

Preheat the oven to 425°F/220°C. Position a rack in the centre of the oven.

Cut off the top 4 cm of the tomatoes, then using a paring knife, cut away the flesh and seeds, leaving the outer layer of the tomato all around to create a tomato bowl (keep the tomato insides for another use – throwing them into tomato soup comes to mind).

Season the insides of the tomatoes with salt and pepper, then spoon 12 tbsp of the rice mixture into each tomato (don't cram it in too tight).

In a small bowl, stir together 1 tablespoon of the rendered chorizo fat with the bread crumbs. Top each tomato with 2 tablespoons of the bread crumb mixture. Arrange on a large rimmed baking sheet and bake until the rice mixture is bubbling and the bread crumbs are golden and toasty, 20 to 25 minutes (the tomatoes may burst or split a little; don't sweat it!).

★ / If you can't find tomatoes of this size, or if you have extra filling, just use a couple more smaller tomatoes and bake for a skootch less time.

CHICKEN & DUMPLINGS

Chicken and dumplings make up everything that my father's side of the family is all about: carbs, meat, and vegetable things that just taste like more meat.

   The pot-pie soup in my last book has become such a kitchen staple for so many of you. It's an amazing feeling, but it also told me that I wasn't going to get away with writing this book without a great chicken soup in it. So here we are: You start with a whole chicken's worth of chicken, which you sear and simmer until it gives all its flavour to the broth. The dumplings are fluffy and doughy and tender and just spongy enough to absorb the savoury soup, and along with the chunks of chicken, turn this into a legit main-course situation.

SERVES 6
ACTIVE TIME / 1 HR
TOTAL TIME / 2 HRS 30 MIN

FOR THE SOUP

1.8 kg bone-in, skin-on chicken parts

Kosher salt and freshly ground black pepper

4 tablespoons vegetable oil

1 bay leaf

2 thyme sprigs, or ½ teaspoon dried thyme

1 rosemary sprig, or ½ teaspoon dried rosemary

3 tablespoons butter

1 large onion, cut into 1-cm dice

2 large carrots, cut into 1-cm dice

2 celery stalks, cut into 1-cm dice

30 g plain flour

1 large potato, peeled and diced

60 ml double cream (optional)

FOR THE DUMPLINGS

1 egg

2 tablespoons milk

2 tablespoons butter, melted

125 g plain flour

2 teaspoons baking powder

¼ teaspoon kosher salt

Something green, for garnish (optional)

MAKE THE SOUP Pat the chicken dry with paper towels and season generously with salt and pepper. In a large casserole dish, heat 2 tablespoons of the oil over medium-high heat. Working in two batches, brown the chicken until golden, about 4 minutes per side. (If the pot is looking a little dark on the bottom, splash in some water and scrape up any browned bits between batches, and keep those juices with the chicken.)

Return all the chicken to the pot and add 2 litres water, the bay leaf, thyme, rosemary, and 1 tablespoon salt.

Bring to a boil, reduce the heat to a gentle simmer, and cook for 1 hour.

Strain the stock through a colander set over a large bowl (there should be about 2 litres liquid; skim off some of the fat if you want). Discard the bay leaf and herb sprigs. Using two forks or a pair of tongs, pick the chicken meat off the bones (discard the bones and skin and set aside).

In the same casserole dish, heat the remaining 2 tablespoons oil and the butter over medium-high heat. Add the onion, carrots and celery and cook, stirring, until the carrots begin to soften, about 6 minutes. Add the flour and cook, stirring, until all the flour has been absorbed and darkens a bit, about 5 minutes. Add the strained stock, the chicken meat and the potato, bring to a boil, then reduce the heat and simmer until the stock thickens, about 20 minutes. Stir in the cream, if using. Season to taste with salt and pepper.

WHILE THE STOCK SIMMERS, MAKE THE DUMPLING DOUGH In a small bowl, whisk together the egg, milk and melted butter. In a large bowl, whisk together the flour, baking powder and salt. Pour the wet ingredients into the flour mixture and stir gently with a fork until just incorporated (the batter will be thick; don't overmix, which could toughen the proceedings). Spoon up 1 tablespoon of the batter and use a second spoon to push it off into the simmering soup. Repeat with the rest of the dough. Cover and cook until the dumplings are fluffy and tender, about 15 minutes.

Divide the soup and dumplings among bowls. Garnish with something green, if you want.

CHEESY CHICKEN MILANESE

Whoever invented Milanese has some serious Jedi-mind-trick stuff going on. I mean, it's a salad. But on top of a fried chicken cutlet. It's like spa food. But it's fried chicken. Maybe you're not as confused by your Milanese emotions as I am.

Anyway, I make sure to remind myself which part of this dish is boss by using both regular and panko bread crumbs for extra crunchy crispy goodness. And I stuff the insides of those cutlets with mozzarella so when you cut into them, they bleed cheese. What spa would serve you that?

SERVES 4
ACTIVE TIME / 40 MIN
TOTAL TIME / 40 MIN

4 boneless, skinless chicken breasts

Kosher salt, freshly ground black pepper and cayenne pepper

125 g plain flour, plus more for 'gluing' the chicken

4 eggs

50 g plain dried bread crumbs*

50 g panko bread crumbs*

100 g shredded whole-milk mozzarella cheese

Rapeseed or vegetable oil, for shallow-frying

150 g baby rocket

200 g cherry tomatoes, halved or quartered

A chunk of Parmigiano-Reggiano cheese

Extra-virgin olive oil (the best you have)

Good-quality balsamic vinegar

Preheat the oven to 325°F/160°C.

Place a chicken breast between two big sheets of plastic wrap. Using the smooth side of a meat pounder or an empty wine bottle (lemme know if you need one), pound the chicken as thin as you can without ripping it to shreds. Season with salt, black pepper and cayenne and repeat with the remaining chicken breasts.

Set up three shallow bowls. Spread out the flour in one and season it liberally with salt, black pepper and cayenne. Place the eggs in the second bowl, season them with salt, and beat them lightly just to combine. Combine the bread crumbs and panko in the third bowl and season with salt and black pepper.

Place ¼ of the mozzarella on one side of each pounded chicken breast, about 5 cm in from the edges. Moisten the edges of the whole breast with water, then sprinkle a little flour all over the edges. Fold the breast over the cheese, pressing on the edges to seal.

Take the folded breast and dip it into the seasoned flour on both sides, shaking off the excess. Move it to the egg and dip in both sides, letting the excess drip off. Transfer to the bread crumbs and press each side into the crumbs. Put the breast on a plate. Repeat the breading procedure with the remaining breasts in the same order: flour, eggs, bread crumbs.

In a large frying pan, heat about 1 cm of oil over medium-high heat. When the oil is hot, carefully lay 2 of the breaded cutlets in the pan and cook until browned and crisp, 2 to 3 minutes. Flip the cutlets and cook until golden brown, another 2 to 3 minutes. Transfer the cutlets to a baking sheet and finish cooking in the oven, about 15 minutes, while you fry the remaining 2 cutlets, adding a little oil to the pan if necessary between batches.

To serve, arrange a cutlet on each of four plates and top each one with a handful of rocket and ¼ of the tomatoes. Use a vegetable peeler to shave some Parm over each cutlet, sprinkle with salt and pepper, and drizzle with olive oil and balsamic.

Using two kinds of bread crumbs makes the chicken extra crunchy and texturey, but you can just double up on one of them.

PAN-SEARED FISH
with Herby Browned Butter

I just realized why I love coriander so frigging much. Coriander is the herb equivalent of yours truly, Christine Diane Teigen. Unlike parsley, which is a take-it-or-leave-it green thing, you have to take a stand on coriander. You either love it or you hate it. Some of you hate it so much you are even allergic to it (or so you claim – still verifying this, but I will give you the benefit of the doubt). So go ahead: Slap the fish in a very hot pan (this helps the fish cook-and-release, rather than stick), let it cook, and bathe it in that herby coriander butter, and if you love it, we can talk.

SERVES 2
ACTIVE TIME / 10 MIN
TOTAL TIME / 20 MIN

4 tablespoons butter, at room temperature

2 tablespoons finely chopped fresh coriander, plus more for garnish

2 cloves garlic, finely minced

1 small shallot, finely minced

Kosher salt and freshly ground black pepper

1 lemon

1 tablespoon rapeseed oil

2 thick white fish fillets, such as halibut or snapper (175-225 g each)

In a small bowl, combine the butter, coriander, garlic, shallot, ¼ teaspoon pepper and salt to taste. Use a Microplane or other fine zester to grate the whole lemon's worth of zest straight into the butter, stir, and set aside. Cut the zested lemon into wedges.

Heat a dry medium frying pan (no oil yet) over medium-high heat until hot but not smoking. Pat the fish dry with a paper towel, then season generously with salt and pepper. Swirl the oil into the pan, let it get shimmery hot, then add the fish (skin-side down if you've got skin-on fish). Let the fish cook and DFWI. (If you move it too soon, the fish will stick and tear.) EXCEPTION: If the fish curls up, gently press down on it with a spatula or a spoon; it'll relax eventually.

Cook until the bottom side is golden and caramelized, 3 to 4 minutes. Using a thin spatula or tongs (be gentle!), turn the fish over, add the herbed butter to the pan, and cook until the other side is just done, about 3 minutes. During the last minute of cooking, you can use a spoon to keep drizzling the butter back over the fish (makes the top a little browner and prettier and buttery-ier).

Put the fish on plates, drizzle with some of the pan sauce, season to taste with salt and pepper, garnish with coriander, and serve with the lemon wedges.

JERK LAMB CHOPS
with Sweet & Salty Banana Rice

I'm sure someone smarter than me has written about this, but there's a lot of connection between Southeast Asian food and Caribbean food. We love our curries, spices, coconut and tropical fruits. And who wouldn't? Everyone should be grateful for the awesome flavours coming from these parts of the world. What would you eat without us?

This jerk lamb is bomb on its own. But the most amazing part of this dish is the bed of sweet, caramelized banana rice the lamb lies on. The bananas will remind you of sweet plantains, but are easier to find.

SERVES 4
ACTIVE TIME / 10 MIN
TOTAL TIME / 25 MIN
(plus up to 8 hrs marinating time)

FOR THE LAMB CHOPS

- **4 tablespoons jerk seasoning (see Note)**
- **2 tablespoons Pickapeppa sauce (see Note) or Worcestershire sauce**
- **6 cloves garlic, finely minced**
- **900 g baby lamb chops, cut into individual chops**
- **1 teaspoon kosher salt**

FOR THE BANANA RICE

- **2 tablespoons vegetable oil**
- **2 small bananas, cut into 5-mm-thick rounds**
- **2 tablespoons sugar**
- **750 g cooked rice**
- **1 teaspoon kosher salt, plus more to taste**
- **A few pinches chopped fresh thyme, for garnish**
- **Lime wedges, for serving**

MAKE THE LAMB CHOPS In a large bowl, combine 2 tablespoons of the jerk seasoning, the Pickapeppa and garlic. Add the lamb chops, and smush around to coat. Marinate in the refrigerator for at least 30 minutes and up to 8 hours.

Heat a griddle or frying pan over medium-high heat until very hot.

Remove the chops from the marinade, pat dry with paper towels, and sprinkle all over with the remaining 2 tablespoons jerk seasoning and the salt. Griddle or fry the chops until nicely seared, 2 to 3 minutes, then flip and cook until medium-rare, another 2 to 3 minutes.

MAKE THE BANANA RICE In a large nonstick frying pan, heat the oil over medium heat. Toss the bananas with the sugar and sauté until slightly caramelized, 2 to 3 minutes. Add the rice and ½ teaspoon of the salt and cook, stirring occasionally (but don't mash up the bananas too much), until very hot, about 3 minutes. Stir in the remaining ½ teaspoon salt, then add more salt until it tastes like a good balance between sweet and salty.

Garnish the lamb with thyme and serve with lime wedges and the rice.

Note / *JERK SEASONING & PICKAPEPPA SAUCE*

Though not as easy to find as, say, paprika, these two seasonings really make this dish. Look for them in the international aisle of a supermarket and if you can't find them . . . hey, isn't that what the Internet is for? Once you have them in your house you'll find all sorts of other uses for them, like marinating a steak (Pickapeppa) or spicing up scrambled eggs or roasted vegetables (jerk seasoning).

VEGGIE COUSCOUS
with Spicy Pine Nuts

John and I have fallen in love with Marrakesh, Morocco. We've visited there every year for the past few years. It's a beautiful city with so much history, gorgeous architecture and design, and the food – ahh, the food! So good! The roasted lamb, the chicken tagine, the *bastilla* (a savoury poultry pie with cinnamon and saffron). The staple that goes with all of this awesomeness is a fluffy couscous, tiny, tiny specks of crushed wheat that is kind of like how rice is for us Asians. I love it with all of the above, but I also love a simple veggie couscous. It may seem so basic and boring, but you know the chef is high quality if they do it right. Do your couscous right!

SERVES 6
ACTIVE TIME / 20 MIN
TOTAL TIME / 40 MIN

FOR THE VEGETABLES

- **3 tablespoons olive oil, plus more for drizzling**
- **1 large onion, chopped**
- **½ teaspoon ground cinnamon**
- **½ teaspoon ground cumin**
- **¼ teaspoon cayenne pepper**
- **Kosher salt**
- **450 g sweet potato, peeled and cut into 3-cm chunks**
- **450 g courgette, cut into 5-cm chunks**
- **375 ml vegetable stock (or chicken stock if you secretly want to sabotage your veggie friends)**

FOR THE SPICY PINE NUTS AND COUSCOUS

- **45 g pine nuts**
- **2 teaspoons plus 1 tablespoon olive oil, plus more for drizzling**
- **¼ teaspoon cayenne pepper**
- **Kosher salt**
- **500 ml vegetable stock, chicken stock, or water**
- **285 g couscous**
- **40 g dried cranberries**
- **15 g chopped fresh coriander, plus more for garnish**
- **Freshly ground black pepper**

COOK THE VEGETABLES In a large (4-litre) saucepan, heat the oil over medium heat. Add the onion and cook, stirring, until tender, about 7 minutes. Add the cinnamon, cumin, cayenne and 1½ teaspoons salt and cook, stirring, for 1 minute. Add the sweet potato, courgette and the stock. Bring to a boil, reduce the heat to a simmer, and cook until the sweet potatoes are easily pierced with a fork, 15 to 20 minutes. Season to taste with salt.

MEANWHILE, MAKE THE SPICY PINE NUTS AND COUSCOUS In a medium saucepan, combine the pine nuts, 2 teaspoons of the oil, the cayenne and a pinch of salt and cook over medium heat, stirring, until the nuts have darkened slightly and are coated in the cayenne, about 4 minutes. Transfer to a plate to cool.

Bring the stock to a boil in the same saucepan. Stir in the couscous, remaining 1 tablespoon oil, and ½ teaspoon salt. Remove from the heat, cover, and let sit for 5 minutes. Uncover, fluff with a fork, add the pine nuts, dried cranberries and coriander, and fluff again. Season to taste with salt and black pepper.

Spoon the couscous on to a platter and top with the vegetables and some of their cooking liquid to moisten. Season with salt and pepper, drizzle with olive oil, and garnish with coriander.

Garlic-Honey PRAWNS

Orange zest is a terrible thing to waste, so I threw some into this fifteen-minute prawn dish along with the orange juice itself. That little hit of bitterness gives this dish a bit of Chinese restaurant-worthy meal cred, if I do say so myself. I use the cornflour trick (diluting some cornflour in liquid before adding it to the sauce to thicken) and the honey trick (to sweeten and make it glossy) and the prawn trick (which is nothing more than . . . deciding to use prawns). By the way, when you see the word *count* in the amount of prawns in a recipe, it's referring to the number per pound; 16–20 count are really pretty big, but other sizes work, too – if they're smaller, just cook them a little less on both sides. Basically, if they're nice and pink on each side by the time you get them out of the pan (before you finish them in the sauce), they're done. The nice thing about having bigger prawns is that you can cook them longer, and get them that beautiful golden brown before you overcook them, but either way, this is gonna be gooooooood.

SERVES 4
ACTIVE TIME / 15 MIN*
TOTAL TIME / 20 MIN

2 medium oranges

3 tablespoons honey

2 tablespoons soy sauce

1 tablespoon unseasoned rice vinegar

1 tablespoon cornflour

450 g large (16–20 count) prawns, peeled and deveined

Kosher salt and freshly ground black pepper

3 tablespoons rapeseed oil

6 cloves garlic, minced

1 tablespoon finely minced fresh ginger

2 spring onions, whites thinly sliced, greens cut into 5-cm lengths

1 teaspoon chilli flakes

Cooked rice, for serving

 If you're not using pre-cleaned prawns, this is more like 25 minutes.

Using a vegetable peeler, pull off a 2.5-cm-wide strip of zest from 1 orange, then finely grate the zest from about half the orange. Reserve both kinds of zest. Juice both oranges into a bowl (you should have just over 125 ml juice; if you have a lot less . . . borrow another orange from somebody). Whisk in the honey, soy sauce and vinegar.

In a small bowl, combine the cornflour with 1 tablespoon of the orange-soy mixture to form a paste, then stir that back into the bowl with the rest of the orange-soy mixture.

Pat the prawns dry with paper towels and season both sides generously with salt and pepper. In the largest frying pan you have, heat 1½ tablespoons of the oil over medium-high heat until shimmering-hot, almost smoking. Add the prawns, spread it out in one layer, DFWI, and cook until the underside is bright pink, 1 to 1½ minutes. Flip and cook 1 minute more, then transfer them to a plate.

Add the remaining 1½ tablespoons oil to the pan. Add the garlic, ginger, spring onion whites and chilli flakes and cook until fragrant, 30 seconds to 1 minute. Add the orange-soy liquid and the strip of orange zest and cook, stirring, until thickened, 1 to 2 minutes. Return the prawns to the pan, add the spring onion greens, and toss to coat with the sauce.

Divide the prawns among bowls, garnish with a few pinches of the grated orange zest, and serve with rice.

SEARED STEAK
with Spicy Garlic-Miso Butter & Same-Pan Asparagus

Miso butter is a gift to us sent from the freaking heavens above. You cannot convince me that the angels don't polish the gates with miso butter on a soft cloth. Honestly, it's perfection on its own, but here we add *garlic and cayenne* because here at *Cravings* we strive for BETTER THAN PERFECTION, OK??? (Don't you hate when people say that sh*t? Or when they give something an '11' on a scale of 1 to 10? Why not 12, then? Is 13 okay? Now you have me wondering why I didn't get an 85 on a 1–10 scale just because you wanted to be dramatic.)

Something happens to you on a spiritual level when you put miso butter on to a hot steak. You feel a genuine sense of both calm and gluttony. It glistens so much that Mufasa himself appears in the juices to tell you to remember who you are. That's a *Lion King* joke I had full confidence in until John told me he didn't get it. They say good jokes don't need to be explained, but I disagree – sometimes the listener is just painfully unaware of really important, slightly obscure animated feature-film scenes.

Where were we? Aaaaah, the asparagus. I highly suggest giving a bite to your friend who doesn't eat green things. It will turn them.

SERVES 2
ACTIVE TIME / 15 MIN
TOTAL TIME / 25 MIN

450 g boneless rib eye steak (about 3 cm thick), NOT trimmed of excess fat

1 teaspoon kosher salt, plus more to taste

½ teaspoon freshly ground black pepper, plus more to taste

1 tablespoon butter

1 clove garlic, finely minced

335 g asparagus, tough bottoms snapped off (see page 139), cut into 5-cm lengths

250 ml low-sodium chicken stock

55 g Spicy Garlic-Miso Butter (recipe follows), or more to taste

Heat a 23-cm cast-iron frying pan over medium-high heat until screaming hot, 6 to 7 minutes. Pat the steak dry with paper towels and season both sides with the salt and pepper. Lay the steak in the pan and DFWI (remember? Don't. F*ck. With. It.). Leave the steak alone for 5 minutes, then flip and DFWI again, another 4 to 5 minutes for medium-rare (longer if you like it more cooked, less if you like it less cooked, but you know that already). Transfer the steak to a chopping board and let it rest.

Pour all but 1 tablespoon of the steak grease out of the pan and return the pan to medium heat. Add the butter, melt it (this happens fast), add the garlic, and cook it until golden, about 30 seconds. Add the asparagus and chicken stock and cook, stirring once in a while, until the stock has evaporated into a glaze and the asparagus is al dente, 2 to 3 minutes (or until a little more cooked – how I like it! – about 5 minutes). Season with salt and pepper.

Slice the steak, arrange it on a serving platter, dollop as much of the miso butter as you want on top, and serve the asparagus alongside.

Spicy Garlic-Miso Butter

MAKES 225 G
ACTIVE TIME / 5 MIN
TOTAL TIME / 5 MIN
(1 hour if you count the butter-freezing time)

100 g butter, at room temperature

70 g white (shiro) miso

2 tablespoons finely minced chives

3 cloves garlic, finely minced

½ teaspoon freshly ground black pepper

Generous pinch of cayenne pepper

In a medium bowl, mash together the butter, miso, chives, garlic, black pepper and cayenne.

You can put the miso butter in a bowl and go to town on it. Or, if you want to be fancy and slice it into discs to put on your steaks, place a piece of plastic wrap over a piece of foil and spread the mixture into a 15 × 5-cm rectangle on the plastic. Fold the foil over the mixture and roll the foil and plastic over the mixture into a loose log. Using the ends to twist, twist the foil into handles and then keep twisting until the butter is compacted into a 10-cm-long log. Chill until ready to use: 1 hour in the freezer or 4 hours in the fridge.

When ready to serve, just open the log and slice off as many butter discs as you like.

STEAK DIANE
with Crispy Onions

My middle name is Diane. I have a bit of a complex about it. I don't know. Diane just isn't, um, cool? I imagine Diane as somebody's frumpy aunt. Peace to all my Dianes out there.

How can we bring Diane back in style? With STEAK! This Diane IS cool. She's full of Stella Artois and Dijon. She's salty and juicy and topped with crispy onions. We all want to be friends with THIS Diane. Invite this Diane to your next dinner party.

SERVES 2 TO 4
ACTIVE TIME / 15 MIN
TOTAL TIME / 45 MIN

450 g fillet steak

Kosher salt and freshly ground black pepper

2 tablespoons rapeseed oil

185 ml Stella Artois or other light lager beer

3 tablespoons butter

35 g minced shallots

3 cloves garlic, minced

185 g white mushrooms, cleaned, trimmed and sliced

125 ml double heavy cream

1 tablespoon Dijon mustard

Chopped fresh thyme, for garnish

Crispy Onions (recipe follows), or Crispy Shallots (page 130), for garnish

Preheat the oven to 350°F/180°C.

Pat the steak dry with paper towels and generously season all over with salt and pepper. In an ovenproof frying pan just large enough to fit the steak, heat the oil over medium-high heat until shimmering hot. Add the steak and brown on all sides, turning several times, 5 to 6 minutes total. Transfer the pan to the oven (or transfer to a small baking dish if you don't have an ovenproof frying pan) and roast until an instant-read thermometer registers 125°F/51°C for medium-rare, about 10 minutes. Transfer the steak to a plate and cover with foil to rest while you make the sauce.

Pour the fat from the pan, add the beer, and bring to a boil over medium heat, scraping up any browned bits on the bottom of the pan. Boil until most of the liquid has evaporated, about 2 minutes. Add the butter, reduce the heat to medium, and cook the shallots and garlic, stirring, until fragrant, about 2 minutes. Add the mushrooms and season generously with salt and pepper. Cook, stirring, until the mushrooms release their water and the juices reduce to a glaze, about 8 minutes. Stir in the cream and the mustard and cook until warmed through. Taste for seasoning.

Slice the steak into medallions, divide among plates, top with the mushroom sauce and garnish with thyme. Serve with the crispy onions.

Crispy Onions

1 large onion

500 ml milk

1.5 l peanut or canola oil, for deep-frying

185 g plain flour

1 teaspoon seasoned salt, plus more to taste

Kosher salt

Use a mandoline to slice the onion into super-thin rings (or use a really sharp knife). Place the onions in a bowl, pour the milk over them, and let them sit there for 1 hour.

In a 4-litre saucepan, heat the oil over medium-high heat to 350°F/180°C. (Use a deep-fry thermometer or test the oil by throwing in a little piece of bread or some bread crumbs; if they sizzle immediately but aren't burning, you're ready.)

In another bowl, mix the flour and seasoned salt. Grab a handful of the onions from the bowl, squeeze them out, and dredge them in the flour. Shake off the excess flour, carefully place the onions into the hot oil, and fry, stirring them a bit so they don't stick to each other, until golden and crisp, 2 to 3 minutes. Use a slotted spoon to transfer the onions to paper towels to drain and season with salt. Repeat with the remaining onions.

MAKES ABOUT 600 G
ACTIVE TIME / 25 MIN
TOTAL TIME / 1 HR 25 MIN
(includes soaking time)

Spice-Rubbed
PARMESAN CHICKEN BREASTS
with Garlicky Sautéed Spinach

I never would have believed this pre-Lulu, but I REALLY appreciate a simple, under-30-minute recipe. But one thing I was ADAMANT about with this cookbook was that I did not want things to be sold as 'easy' if it tasted . . . well . . . easy. I wanted every bite to taste like your heart and soullllll were poured into it for hours, even if only you know that all you did was mince some garlic for a spice rub, throw cheese on a chicken breast, and slide it into the oven.

But you did. That's all you freakin' did. But you took the time to find a nice, thick chicken breast to make it effortlessly juicy and a nice Parm to get all melty toasty on the top. *That* is the love part.

I don't think there is a recipe in here I could enjoy on a more consistent basis than this one. Serve it over my buttery Golden Onion Rice Pilaf (page 131) and make sure alllllll those spicy juices drip down into every single beautiful curvaceous nook of the rice pile.

SERVES 4
ACTIVE TIME / 5 MIN
TOTAL TIME / 30 MIN

- **60 ml olive oil, plus more for the baking sheet**
- **6 cloves garlic, finely minced**
- **1½ teaspoons paprika, plus more for sprinkling**
- **1 teaspoon kosher salt**
- **½ teaspoon finely ground black pepper**
- **¼ teaspoon cayenne pepper**
- **4 boneless, skinless chicken breasts, patted dry**
- **120 g cups finely grated Parmigiano-Reggiano cheese**
- **Garlicky Sautéed Spinach (recipe follows), for serving**

Preheat the oven to 400°F/200°C. Line a baking sheet with foil and grease the foil with olive oil.

In a small bowl, combine the oil, garlic, paprika, salt, black pepper and cayenne and rub it all over the chicken. Arrange the chicken on the lined baked sheet. Sprinkle the Parm all over the chicken.

Bake until the cheese starts to turn golden and the chicken is just about finished, 15 to 17 minutes. Remove the chicken from the oven, crank up the grill and grill the chicken until the top is browned and sizzling, 3 to 4 minutes. Let rest for 5 minutes before serving. (Don't forget to scrape up the crispy Parmesan cheese from the foil, unless it's burnt black.) Sprinkle with paprika and serve with garlicky sautéed spinach.

Garlicky Sautéed Spinach

SERVES 4
ACTIVE TIME / 10 MIN
TOTAL TIME / 10 MIN

60 ml olive oil

4 cloves garlic, thinly sliced

450 g baby spinach

¼ teaspoon chilli flakes

Kosher salt and freshly ground black pepper

In a large frying pan, heat the oil over medium-low heat. Add the garlic and cook, stirring, until it softens and turns light golden, 2 to 3 minutes. Increase the heat to medium and add the spinach in batches, cooking down and wilting between batches, until it's all wilted but still bright green. Add the chilli flakes with the last batch of spinach. Season with salt and black pepper to taste.

BRAISED SHORT RIBS
with Maple–Brown Butter Sweet Potato Mash

We all want to act like we're classy sometimes. Like, we know which fork goes with which course. We know which side of the plate the bread and drink go on. We know exactly how to put our napkin in our lap. I don't know much about any of this stuff, but I do know that every classy charity gala dinner John and I go to has a short rib on the menu. Usually with a mashed potato and some string beans. I don't know why this is true, but it is.

So I figure the best way to make a classy meal that everybody will love is to make a tender, flavourful short rib. Of course, I had to add some spice to it, and my mashed potato is made from sweet potatoes. But go ahead, class it up! Have a short rib.

SERVES 6
ACTIVE TIME / 45 MIN
TOTAL TIME / 3 HRS 30 MIN

FOR THE RIBS

- **2 teaspoons cayenne pepper**
- **2 teaspoons paprika**
- **Kosher salt and freshly ground black pepper**
- **6 tablespoons rapeseed oil**
- **4 pounds beef short ribs, cut English-style***
- **4 large carrots, cut into 5-cm pieces**
- **3 celery stalks, cut into 5-cm pieces**
- **400 g frozen pearl (silverskin) onions, thawed, or 1 large onion, cut into 1-inch dice**
- **1½ tablespoons plain flour**
- **1 tablespoon tomato paste**
- **375 ml bottled beer (any kind)**
- **2 tablespoons light brown sugar**
- **6 Roma (plum) tomatoes, diced, or 2 (400-g) cans diced tomatoes**
- **500 ml beef stock**
- **2 bay leaves**

FOR THE SWEET POTATO MASH

- **900 g orange sweet potatoes (about 6 large)**
- **6 tablespoons butter**
- **60 ml maple syrup**
- **Kosher salt and freshly ground black pepper**

MAKE THE RIBS Preheat the oven to 325°F/160°C. Arrange the racks so there's room for both the sweet potato tray and your braising pot.

In a small bowl, combine the cayenne, paprika, 1 teaspoon salt and 1 teaspoon black pepper. Rub all of the meaty parts of the ribs with the rub, then wash your hands, because the cayenne is not gonna feel good if you forget about it on your fingers.

In a large casserole dish, heat 4 tablespoons of the oil over medium-high heat until shimmering-hot. Add the ribs and brown all over until golden, turning every few minutes to brown all three sides, 10 minutes total. (If they won't all fit comfortably, work in batches.) Transfer the ribs to a platter, pour the fat out of the pot, then carefully wipe out the pot with a wad of paper towel (some of the spices in the pot are probably burnt and you don't want to be involved with them any more).

★ So apparently 'English-style' is a nice way of saying caveman-style. I mean, you want big hunks of meat attached to 5- or 7-cm-long bones. (It's one bone cut into smaller pieces; not Korean-style, which are thin slices across a few bones.)

CONTINUES

Add the remaining 2 tablespoons oil to the pot, still over medium-high heat. Add the carrots, celery and onions and cook, stirring occasionally, until the carrots and celery begin to soften, about 5 minutes. Add the flour and cook, stirring, until it disappears into the vegetables and the flour browns a drop, about 2 minutes. Add the tomato paste and cook, stirring, for 1 minute. Add the beer and scrape up the browned bits at the bottom of the pot using a metal spoon. Bring to a boil and cook until the liquid has reduced by half and thickened, 5 to 6 minutes. Stir in the brown sugar. Add the tomatoes, beef stock, bay leaves and 2 teaspoons salt.

Bring to a boil, then return the short ribs to the pot, bone-side up. Cover, transfer to the oven, and bake until the meat is super tender and the liquid has thickened, 2½ to 3 hours.

Carefully remove the ribs from the liquid (they might fall apart on you; that's OK, but be gentle!). Remove the bones from the meat, then cover the meat with foil to keep warm. Set a colander over a large bowl and gently dump the vegetables and liquid into the colander. Skim the fat off the liquid and season to taste with salt and pepper. Return the vegetables to the strained liquid and cover to keep warm.

MAKE THE SWEET POTATO MASH After the ribs have been baking for about 45 minutes, pierce the sweet potatoes all over with a fork, arrange them on a baking sheet and bake until tender, 1¼ to 1½ hours. Remove them from the oven and let cool for 10 minutes.

While the potatoes are cooling, in a small saucepan, heat the butter over medium heat until browned and toasted, 4 to 5 minutes. (Be careful not to burn it! It should just start to smell nutty.) Add the maple syrup and 1 teaspoon salt and cook for 30 seconds. Remove from the heat and cover to keep warm.

Remove the skins from the sweet potatoes, place the flesh in a large bowl, add the maple-butter mixture, and mash until smooth. (If you want them super smooth you can do this in a food processor.) Season to taste with salt and pepper.

Scoop the mashed potatoes on to a serving platter and serve the ribs on top. Pour some of the gravy on top and serve the rest of the gravy with the braising vegetables, if you want.

Ron's Hobo
BURGER DINNERS

Wait, are we allowed to say 'hobo' any more? I don't get mad when John's granny says 'oriental', so maybe my dad, who is seventy-nine years old, gets a pass for calling these things 'hobo dinners'. Anyway, this little dish of magic includes ingredients you can find anywhere, wrapped into a tight little foil package you could essentially cook over any heat source: an open flame, a running car engine, an oven. An oven is preferred.

When I was growing up, Dad made these every Friday night, stacking up carrots, potatoes and onions on a beef patty and squeezing eight seconds' worth of ketchup on top. Prep time was around five minutes, and nothing made me happier than eagerly opening up my little meat package (too quickly) and burning off my fingertips. This recipe is . . . life changing. Because now I can commit any crime I want without leaving fingerprints.

SERVES 4
ACTIVE TIME / 15 MIN
TOTAL TIME / 45 MIN

1 large onion

1 large potato, scrubbed

Kosher salt and freshly ground black pepper

2 tablespoons rapeseed oil

450 g ground beef

3 cloves garlic, minced

½ teaspoon paprika

¼ teaspoon cayenne pepper

1 teaspoon Worcestershire sauce

1 egg, beaten

15 g fresh bread crumbs (see page 178)

185 ml ketchup

1 carrot, cut into thin coins

4 tablespoons butter, melted

Preheat the oven to 450°F/230°C.

Cut four 1-cm-thick slices from the centre of the onion. Cut four 1-cm-thick slices of potato on the bias, so they're nice and long, and poke them a few times with a fork. Season both sides of the onion and potato with salt and pepper. Heat the oil in a large frying pan over medium-low heat, arrange the potatoes and onions in the pan, and cook until golden and softened, about 5 minutes per side.

In a large bowl, gently combine the beef, garlic, 1 teaspoon salt, ½ teaspoon black pepper, the paprika, cayenne, Worcestershire, egg and bread crumbs, using your hands, and form the mixture into 4 equal-size patties, about 12 cm in diameter and 1.5 cm thick.

Tear four large sheets of heavy-duty aluminium foil. Squirt about 1 tablespoon of ketchup on to the centre of each piece of foil and top with a burger patty. Top each patty with a potato slice, followed by an onion slice, and arrange thin slices of carrot all around the burger. Whisk together the melted butter with the remaining 125 ml ketchup and pour the mixture evenly over the packets. Fold up and seal the foil packets, place them on a baking sheet, and bake until the potato is cooked through and the burgers are tender and juicy, 20 minutes. Transfer each packet to a plate, cut the packets open, and serve hot.

SWEET MISO-BUTTER COD
with Sugar Snap Peas

If you've ever heard of the restaurant Nobu, you know that their miso cod is basically legendary in the food world. Sure, a lot of restaurants have knocked it off for decades, but Nobu made it the go-to. He soaks it for dayyyyys in some secret sweet miso, then blackens it under a grill. It is, essentially, candy fish.

Well, we don't have Nobu's secret miso marinade. And even if we did, we wouldn't have the time to marinate it for days. But I'd be willing to bet NOOOOOO one you know will even remember *that* miso cod once *this* is placed in their face. You get that miso hit with some brown sugar sweetness and, oh yeah, *butter*. Did I mention we're using the same gold-standard, award-winning (I bought an old trophy at Goodwill) spicy miso butter as the miso rib eye on page 197???

And the peas just look and taste dope in this sauce. Some things are simple like that. Try not to burn your tongue licking the sauce off the grill pan.

SERVES 2
ACTIVE TIME / 10 MIN
TOTAL TIME / 20 MIN

2 skinless centre-cut (thick) fillets cod (170 g each)

Kosher salt and freshly ground black pepper

6 tablespoons Spicy Garlic-Miso Butter (page 198), at room temperature

50 g light brown sugar

60 ml sake

225 g sugar snap peas, ends trimmed (see Tip)

Preheat the grill to medium-low.

Season the fish liberally with salt and pepper. In a 23-cm ovenproof nonstick frying pan, combine the miso butter, brown sugar, sake and 1 tablespoon water. Heat over medium heat, stirring to incorporate, until bubbling.

Place the fish in the pan and cook until the bottom 1 cm of the fillets is opaque, about 4 minutes. Spoon some of the sauce over the fish and throw the peas in the pan. Place under the grill and grill until the top is nice and caramelized and even a little charred in spots, another 4 to 8 minutes (make sure to keep watching the fish; if it's burning too fast, reduce the heat or put the pan on a lower rack). Divide the fish, sauce and peas between two plates.

Tip / *SNAP!*

Sometimes sugar snap peas have flossy strings that you don't really want to eat. Taste one or two, and if there's no string, just trim the ends; if there *are* stringy things in there, remove them by finding the ends of the peas, snapping them, and pulling; the strings should come right out of the seam.

Simple 'Pan-Fried'
BROKEN LASAGNA

The first recipe I made for my last book was courgette lasagna, and while it's still one of my favourites, it's laughably time-consuming, between the six-hour-simmering sauce and the layers and layers of must-be-roasted-beforehand courgette strips. For *this* book's lasagna, I went for max flavour with minimum effort. The sauce is easier and faster, and this time you get to take out all your aggressions by breaking the pasta sheets and sticking them into your pan with the sauce and cheese. You don't even have to make neat layers! It's like a lasagna that let itself go . . . which is obviously the best kind of lasagna, right?

SERVES 8
ACTIVE TIME / 40 MIN
TOTAL TIME / 1 HR 45 MIN

FOR THE SAUCE

2 tablespoons extra-virgin olive oil

350 g ground beef

350 g ground pork

1 large onion, finely diced

9 cloves garlic, minced

50 g tomato paste

4 (400-g) cans crushed tomatoes

30 g shredded fresh basil

¼ teaspoon chilli flakes

Kosher salt and freshly ground black pepper

FOR THE LASAGNA

500 g ricotta cheese

345 g shredded mozzarella cheese

60 g finely grated Parmigiano-Reggiano cheese

30 g shredded fresh basil

¾ teaspoon kosher salt

½ teaspoon freshly ground black pepper

170 g no-boil lasagna sheets broken into 5-cm pieces

MAKE THE SAUCE In a casserole dish, heat the oil over medium-high heat. Add the beef and pork and cook, breaking up the meat into tiny pieces with a wooden spoon, until no longer pink, 5 to 6 minutes. (Don't stress over it getting brown.) Transfer to a bowl.

Drain off and discard all but enough of the fat from the pot to slick the bottom. Add the onion and cook until tender and translucent, 7 to 8 minutes. Add the garlic and cook 1 additional minute. Add the tomato paste and cook, stirring, for 2 minutes. Return the meat to the pot along with the tomatoes, basil, chilli flakes, 1 tablespoon salt, and 1 teaspoon black pepper. Bring to a boil, then reduce the heat and simmer until slightly thickened, about 45 minutes. Season to taste with salt and pepper.

Preheat the oven to 375°F/190°C.

BUILD AND BAKE THE LASAGNA In a large bowl, combine the ricotta, mozzarella, Parm, basil, salt and pepper.

Spoon 250 ml of the sauce into the bottom of a large (30-cm), deep (5-cm) ovenproof frying pan. Add a layer of pasta (since it's broken you can kind of just set it into a layer without worrying about how exactly it will fit together), then a layer of sauce, then a layer of dollops of the cheese mixture. Repeat layers of pasta (pressing down on it to compact everything), sauce and cheese until the pan is full, topping with a final layer of sauce and then dollops of cheese at the very top.

Put a rimmed baking sheet in the oven and put the pan on top of it (this prevents burny drips in the bottom of your oven). Bake until bubbling, about 45 minutes.

Coconut SHORT RIB CURRY (Beef Rendang)

I know this book could have been titled *Cravings2: Loco for Coco*, and I am just fine with that. There are – count 'em – two types of coconut in this recipe, and if I could have squeezed in a third you know I would have. I've never met a curry I didn't like, but this one, from Malaysia, is *really* amazing. You blend pretty much all my favourite herbs and spices (lemongrass and ginger and garlic, oh my!) into a paste that you simmer for hours, eventually pretty much frying short rib meat in its own fat into a dark and, to be quite honest, pretty fugly pile of greatness. Like, this baby is nottttt photogenic. But I know you know better than to let its appearance fool you.

SERVES 4
ACTIVE TIME / 30 MIN
TOTAL TIME / 4 HRS

- **4 large shallots, roughly chopped**
- **8-cm piece fresh ginger, peeled and roughly chopped**
- **2 stalks fresh lemongrass, peeled and roughly chopped (see Tip, page 99)**
- **3 fresh or dried kaffir lime leaves (see page 147)**
- **6 cloves garlic**
- **1 tablespoon chilli flakes**
- **2 teaspoons ground turmeric**
- **1½ teaspoons ground coriander**
- **1 teaspoon ground cinnamon**

- **Kosher salt**
- **2 tablespoons vegetable oil**
- **900 g boneless beef short ribs, cut into large cubes**
- **Freshly ground black pepper**
- **1 (400 ml) can full-fat coconut milk, shaken**
- **50 g brown sugar**
- **30 g unsweetened finely shredded coconut**
- **Cooked rice, for serving**
- **Chopped fresh coriander or spring onions and finely sliced chillies, for garnish**

In a blender or food processor, combine the shallots, ginger, lemongrass, kaffir lime leaves, garlic, chilli flakes, turmeric, coriander, cinnamon, 2 teaspoons salt and 60 ml water. Process until smooth, adding a little more water if necessary to keep the stuff moving in the machine.

In a large heavy-bottomed pot or casserole dish with a tight-fitting lid, heat the oil over medium-high heat. Season the meat generously with salt and pepper. Brown the meat (DFWI) until a crust forms, 4 minutes per side, then remove it to a plate. (Do this in batches if necessary to not crowd the pan, and in between batches, splash in some water, scrape up the browned bits, and add those juices to the seared meat on the plate.)

Add the blended spice mixture to the pot and cook, stirring, until the mixture darkens and is very fragrant, 2 to 3 minutes. Add the coconut milk and brown sugar and stir until the sugar is dissolved. Return the meat to the pot. Bring it to a low boil, reduce the heat to a gentle simmer, cover and cook for 2 hours. (Check in on the pot every once in a while to make sure it's not totally dry; if it is, splash some water in there.)

Stir in the shredded coconut, cover and cook until the meat is really soft and falling apart, another 1 hour. Uncover, increase the heat to medium-high and cook, stirring, until any liquid is reduced and the meat is coated in a thick paste (it's not really super saucey). Serve with rice and garnish with chillies, coriander or spring onions.

CRISPY-SKINNED CHICKEN
with Lemon-Rosemary Pan Sauce

Lemons and rosemary are your friends here. They take a buttery sauce spiked with salty chicken juice and crank it up to the level of world-beating recipe. And the fact that everything happens to these chicken boobies in one pan makes it extra CT-approved in the age of running toddlers and husbands who go on tour, leaving their wife and child back at home while they work 90 minutes a day.

SERVES 2 TO 4
ACTIVE TIME / 15 MIN
TOTAL TIME / 35 MIN

FOR THE CHICKEN

- 2 large bone-in, skin-on chicken breasts (340 g each), trimmed of extra fat
- Kosher salt and freshly ground black pepper
- 2 cloves garlic, minced
- 1 teaspoon chopped fresh rosemary, or ½ teaspoon dried
- Finely grated zest of ½ lemon
- ¼ teaspoon chilli flakes
- 2 tablespoons extra-virgin olive oil

FOR THE SAUCE

- 6 cloves garlic, minced
- ¼ teaspoon chilli flakes
- ½ teaspoon chopped fresh rosemary, or ¼ teaspoon dried
- 125 ml chicken stock
- 2 tablespoons double cream
- 1 tablespoon fresh lemon juice
- 4 tablespoons butter, cut into chunks and chilled
- Kosher salt and freshly ground black pepper

MAKE THE CHICKEN Preheat the oven to 425°F/220°C. Pat the chicken dry with paper towels and season generously with salt and black pepper. In a small bowl, combine the garlic, rosemary, lemon zest, chilli flakes and 1 tablespoon of the oil. Gently tuck half the mixture under the skin of each breast.

In a large ovenproof frying pan, heat the remaining 1 tablespoon oil over medium heat (until just-shimmering hot). Swirl the oil around the pan, then add the chicken skin-side down and DFWI. Cook without moving (it's OK to press it down gently to make sure it lies flat) until the skin is browned, 6 to 8 minutes. Flip the chicken, move the pan into the oven, and cook until the chicken is cooked through, about 20 minutes. Transfer the chicken to a plate.

MAKE THE SAUCE Using an oven mitt, carefully put the pan back over medium heat (remember, it's hot!). Add the garlic, chilli flakes and rosemary to the drippings in the pan and cook, stirring, until fragrant, about 1 minute. Add the chicken stock and cream, bring to a boil and cook, stirring and scraping any browned bits off the bottom of the pan, until the stock reduces and is thick, 2 to 3 minutes. Add the lemon juice, then whisk in the butter one chunk at a time until the sauce thickens and is glossy. Season to taste with salt and black pepper.

Pour the sauce over the chicken or serve it on the side.

Sesame Salmon
SOBA SALAD

I created this dish because I loved the title. Actually, I came up with it because, almost two years and thousands of finger-wagging comments later, I am *still* convinced that my unconventional method for cooking salmon and creating crispy skin at the same time is the key to fish bliss. Keep a mango in the house and a pack of soba (think of them as Japanese spaghetti), and you've got this one. And if you don't care for crispy salmon skin, you can use crispy wonton wrappers and feed the salmon skins to your dog. They love them!

SERVES 4 AS A MAIN
DISH OR 6 TO 8 AS AN
APPETIZER
ACTIVE TIME / 30 MIN
TOTAL TIME / 30 MIN

225 g soba noodles

3 tablespoons sesame oil

2 tablespoons rapeseed oil

Finely grated zest of 1 lime

3 tablespoons fresh lime juice (from about 1½ limes), plus more as needed

2 tablespoons unseasoned rice vinegar

1½ tablespoons honey

Kosher salt

2 skin-on salmon fillets (170 g each), patted dry

Freshly ground black pepper

1 firm-ripe medium mango, peeled and cut into thin strips

1 medium cucumber, skin on, peeled into ribbons*

4 spring onions, chopped, plus more for garnish

1 medium fresh red or green chilli, thinly sliced

3 tablespoons toasted sesame seeds (black or white), or more to taste

★ / Or just chop the cucumber if you feel like it.

★★ / This salad really drinks up the dressing. If you've found the flavours faded before serving, jack them up with some extra lime juice and salt.

Set up a large bowl with ice water. Bring a medium pot of water to a boil. Cook the soba until tender but not mushy, about 6 minutes. Drain, rinse well and transfer to the ice water, swishing the noodles around a bit until the water becomes slightly cloudy (that's how you know the starch has been washed off). Drain the noodles very well (pat dry with a clean towel if you're OCD like that).

In a small bowl, whisk together the sesame oil, rapeseed oil, lime zest, lime juice, vinegar, honey and 1 teaspoon salt.

Heat the grill to medium.

Season the salmon generously with salt and pepper. Arrange the salmon, skin-side up, on the grill pan, lined with foil, and grill until the salmon is just cooked through, 6 to 7 minutes. Leave the grill on but reduce the temp to low.

Let the salmon cool until you can handle it (can you handle it????). Peel off the skin and arrange it on the grill pan. Grill the salmon skins until crisped and browned but not burnt, 2 to 3 minutes (this is their tanning booth). Meanwhile, separate the salmon flesh into big bites.

In a large bowl, combine the soba noodles, mango, cucumber, spring onions, chilli and dressing and toss gently.**

Divide the soba salad among bowls, top with the salmon chunks, and break up some of the salmon skin over each bowl. Sprinkle with the sesame seeds and spring onions.

GRIDDLED PORTOBELLOS
with Chimichurri

I hate parsley and you can't stop me. I know like half the world is allergic to coriander, but that's the food of the gods as far as I'm concerned, and parsley to me is like edible weeds. Every bite of parsley is like God punishing me for something I did as a child. It's like if you took a beautiful Bentley (delicious food) and put family-stick-figure stickers (the parsley) on it. When my grocery delivery brings me parsley instead of coriander, I take it as a personal attack on my family. When my dad left us he said he was going out to get parsley. My horrible ex-boyfriend loved parsley. I don't know. Anyhow, chimichurri normally is like 50 per cent parsley, but my chimichurri is all coriander, spring onions, garlic, shallots, chillies, oil and vinegar and therefore it's perfect: herby and oniony and tart. (OK, I know there are four recipes in this book with parsley – don't @ me.)

SERVES 3 AS A VEGGIE
MAIN COURSE OR 4 AS AN
APPETIZER OR SIDE
ACTIVE TIME / 15 MIN
TOTAL TIME / 50 MIN

FOR THE PARSLEY-LESS (BUT STILL DELICIOUS) CHIMI

- **85 ml red wine vinegar**
- **85 ml extra-virgin olive oil**
- **3 tablespoons finely chopped shallots**
- **3 cloves garlic, thinly sliced**
- **2 spring onions, finely minced**
- **1 tablespoon finely minced fresh red chilli, or 1½ teaspoons chilli flakes, or to taste**
- **15 g finely chopped fresh coriander**
- **¾ teaspoon kosher salt, or more to taste**
- **¼ teaspoon freshly ground black pepper**

FOR THE MUSHROOMS

- **560 g portobello mushroom caps (6 to 8 caps, or about 750 g with the stems)**
- **Kosher salt and freshly ground black pepper**
- **Thinly sliced spring onions, for garnish**

MAKE THE CHIMI In a small bowl, stir together the vinegar, oil, shallots, garlic, spring onions, chil, coriander, salt and black pepper.

PREPARE THE MUSHROOMS Set the mushrooms gill-side up. Use a spoon to scoop out the gills and discard them. (OK, you don't *have* to do this, but they're prettier and don't stain everything black if you do, and they get juicier that way.)

Arrange the mushrooms on a baking sheet or in a baking dish and rub all over with about half the chimi. Marinate at room temperature for 30 minutes.

Preheat a griddle pan over medium-high heat until really hot but not smoking.

Season the shrooms with salt and pepper (just as you would a steak) and griddle them, domed-side down, until grill marks form, 4 to 5 minutes. Flip and griddle, basting a couple of times with the marinade, until charred on both sides and tender all the way through, an additional 3 to 5 minutes. (If you don't mind babying them, flipping the mushrooms a couple of times actually helps make them extra juicy.)

Put the mushrooms on a cutting board, let them rest for a couple of minutes, then slice into thick slices. Serve them with the remaining chimi and garnish with spring onions.

Sweet SOY-GLAZED PORK CHOPS
with Tangy Buttery Courgettes

Fact: There is a coyote roaming around the hills behind our house. Fact: Every time we use our griddle pan, we set off the alarm system, and the best way to get that sucker to chill is to slide open the back door. So making these sweet, juicy, done-before-you-blinked pork chops sets off a debate every time: Are they worth the possibility of a *wild dog* hanging out in our living room? If you factor in the butter-soy veg and how quickly the whole dinner comes together, I think the answer is yes. Maybe we'll just make our coyote a plate and leave it by the back door. He is our coyote now.

SERVES 2 TO 4
ACTIVE TIME / 10 MIN
TOTAL TIME / 30 MIN

4 tablespoons soy sauce

2 tablespoons rapeseed oil

1 tablespoon light brown sugar

3 cloves garlic, minced

Kosher salt and freshly ground black pepper

4 thin-cut bone-in pork chops (115 g each)

2 medium courgettes (about 140 g each), halved lengthwise

1 small onion, cut into 6 wedges

1 red or green jalapeño, halved lengthwise and seeded

2 tablespoons butter, cut into small chunks

2 teaspoons distilled white vinegar

In a 3.5-litre size zip-top plastic bag, combine 3 tablespoons of the soy sauce, 1 tablespoon of the oil, the brown sugar, garlic, and a generous pinch each of salt and pepper. Add the pork chops and smush them around to cover with the marinade.

Preheat a griddle pan over medium-high heat.

Brush the courgettes, onion and jalapeño with the remaining 1 tablespoon oil and season generously with salt and pepper. Reduce the heat to medium and griddle until the courgettes and onion are tender and charred on both sides, 7 to 8 minutes per side. While the vegetables are cooking, in a medium bowl, combine the butter, vinegar and the remaining 1 tablespoon soy sauce.

Transfer the griddled vegetables to a chopping board and right away cut them into bite-size pieces (don't burn your fingers! Use tongs or a fork. Be safe, be smart, stay in school). While still hot, drop them in the bowl with the butter-soy-vinegar, toss and cover with foil to keep warm.

Remove the pork chops from the marinade and griddle until just cooked, 1 to 2 minutes per side. Serve the chops with the vegetables.

SHAKE & BAKE CHICKEN
with Hot Honey

'First you shake. Then you bake . . . . And I helped!!' I love fried chicken, but sometimes I'm feeling nostalgic. Sometimes I want to go back to the old-school Shake 'n Bake commercial where the little girl helped Grandma secretly bake 'fried' chicken, then spilled the beans to her parents. These commercials worked on my family. We went right to the grocery store so we could buy boxes of Shake 'n Bake to make in our kitchen in Snohomish, Washington. It was a simpler time. And I f*ckin' helped!

SERVES 4 TO 6
ACTIVE TIME / 15 MIN
TOTAL TIME / 1 HR
(plus up to 4 hrs marinating time)

FOR THE CHICKEN MARINADE
125 ml olive oil

60 ml red wine vinegar

2 cloves garlic, minced

1 teaspoon onion powder

1 teaspoon sugar

1 teaspoon dried basil

1 teaspoon dried oregano

½ teaspoon dried thyme

½ teaspoon kosher salt

¼ teaspoon freshly ground black pepper

¼ teaspoon cayenne pepper

1.5 kg bone-in, skin-on chicken pieces

FOR THE BREAD CRUMBS
135 g plain dried bread crumbs or fine cornflake crumbs*

60 g plain flour

1 teaspoon paprika

1 teaspoon sugar

1 teaspoon kosher salt

¼ teaspoon freshly ground black pepper

Dash of cayenne pepper

Oil, for the baking dish

Hot Honey (recipe follows), for serving

Preheat the oven to 425°F/220°C.

MARINATE THE CHICKEN In a small bowl, whisk together the oil, vinegar, garlic, onion powder, sugar, dried herbs, salt, black pepper and cayenne. Transfer to a huge zip-top plastic bag or bowl. Add the chicken and smush around to coat. Marinate in the fridge for at least 30 minutes and up to 4 hours.

MAKE THE BREAD CRUMBS In a large zip-top plastic bag, combine the bread crumbs, flour, paprika, sugar, salt, black pepper and cayenne.

Working with one piece at a time, remove the chicken from the marinade, shake off the excess, place it in the bag of crumbs, and shake it, pressing on the bag a little to make the coating stick to the chicken.

Lightly oil a large (25 × 38 cm) glass or metal baking dish and arrange the chicken, skin-side down, in the dish. (You want to go top-side down because you're going to flip it later for serving.) Bake for 25 minutes, then take the dish out, flip the chicken and bake until the top is golden and crispy, another 20 to 25 minutes. Serve it with hot honey.

★ You can buy cornflake crumbs, or if you're feeling your pyjamas and don't want to leave the house, pulse cornflakes in a food processor until they reach bread-crumb consistency.

Hot Honey /

MAKES 250 ML
ACTIVE TIME / 8 MIN
TOTAL TIME / 8 MIN

250 ml honey
1 tablespoon chilli flakes

In a small saucepan, bring the chilli flakes and honey
to a low simmer over low heat and cook for 5 minutes.
Remove from the heat, cool and use.

One-Pot SEAFOOD STEW with Pan-Fried Flatbread

OK. This is going to be the most unrelatable thing in this cookbook, but here goes. I was inspired to make this stew by the glaciers of Iceland. Really. I was out there for an UGG photo shoot (THEY'RE COMFY AND YOU KNOW IT) and they had this incredible, bearded hunk of a man-chef cook for us for a shot that I will never, ever forget. I mean, I forget the photos, but I will never forget his soup and the bread technique that went along with it.

We were a few feet from the ocean, and he piled lava rocks over a roaring little fire and literally randomly grabbed whatever shellfish were poking out from the sand. He rolled dough in his hands and flattened it into a hot pan. It was a thing of beauty. We ate it then and there, toasting our he-man with a crisp white wine. Oh, it was glorious.

The broth for this soup is a delicious tomato Jacuzzi that you heat up until all bubbling and warm, and it would be great by itself, but then at the last minute you add all this fresh seafood so it's perfectly cooked and flavours the broth. The simple, pan-fried flatbread is perfect with it and it also does an amazing thing: It makes me feel like I can make bread.

SERVES 8
ACTIVE TIME / 20 MIN*
TOTAL TIME / 1 HR

60 ml olive oil, plus more for drizzling

1 fennel bulb, trimmed and cored (fronds reserved) and thinly sliced

1 medium onion, chopped

2 medium carrots, chopped

2 large celery stalks, cut into 1-cm dice

3 cloves garlic, minced

Kosher salt

1 teaspoon freshly ground black pepper

½ teaspoon chilli flakes

125 ml dry white wine

1 lemon

2 (400-g) cans chopped tomatoes

1.5 l stock (vegetable, fish, or chicken)

1 medium potato, peeled and cut into 1-cm dice

335 g scallops

335 g large (16–20 count) peeled and deveined large prawns

335 g skinned white fish fillet, such as cod or snapper, cut into 2-cm pieces

Pan-Fried Flatbread (recipe follows)

In a large (5- or 6-litre) heavy soup pot, heat the oil over medium-high heat. Add the fennel, onion, carrots and celery and cook, stirring, until the vegetables begin to soften, about 5 minutes. Add the garlic, 1 teaspoon salt, ½ teaspoon of the black pepper and the chilli flakes and cook, stirring, for 1 minute.

Add the wine and cook until most of the liquid evaporates, about 5 minutes. Peel a 2-cm-wide strip of zest from the lemon with a vegetable peeler. Cut the rest of the lemon into wedges. Add the tomatoes, their juices, the stock, the potato, lemon zest strip, 1 teaspoon salt and the remaining ½ teaspoon pepper. Bring to a boil, then reduce to a simmer and cook, stirring occasionally, until the vegetables are tender, about 30 minutes. If the stew seems too thick, add another 250 ml stock or water.

About 5 minutes before serving, remove the lemon zest strip. Season the scallops, prawns and fish with salt. Gently stir the seafood into the stew and simmer until opaque and just cooked through, just a few minutes (keep an eye on the seafood rather than the clock). Season the stew to taste with salt.

Top with the fennel fronds, drizzle with olive oil, and serve with the lemon wedges and the flatbread.

 If you don't buy already-cleaned shrimp, this is more like 40 minutes.

Pan-Fried Flatbread

MAKES 6 BREADS
ACTIVE TIME / 30 MIN
TOTAL TIME / 2 HRS 30 MIN

1 teaspoon active dry yeast

1 tablespoon sugar

170 ml warm water

280 g plain flour, plus more for your hands, the table, everything, and everywhere

¾ teaspoon baking soda

¼ teaspoon baking powder

1 teaspoon kosher salt, plus more for sprinkling

60 ml whole-milk yogurt or sour cream, at room temperature

2 tablespoons olive oil

3 cloves garlic, chopped

1 tablespoon chopped fresh rosemary (sorry, dried won't work here—it'll burn on contact)

6 tablespoons butter, melted

In a medium glass bowl, whisk the yeast, sugar and water together with a fork and let it sit until foamy, about 10 minutes. The yeast is alive. It's eating the sugar and burping up the foam. THIS IS BIOLOGY, PEOPLE.

In a large bowl, whisk together the flour, baking soda, baking powder and salt. Add the yogurt and olive oil to the yeast liquid, then pour this into the flour mixture. Knead it right in the bowl until it just comes together but is really sticky, about 2 minutes. (You're going to want to add more flour to make it less sticky. Don't do it.)

Cover the bowl with plastic wrap and let the dough rise in a warm place until doubled in size, about 2 hours. Uncover and turn the dough out on to a well-floured surface, and have an extra pile of flour ready for use. Divide the dough into 6 pieces. Flour your work surface and use a rolling pin to gently stretch the dough into rounds 13 cm in diameter and 5 mm thick, sprinkling some garlic and rosemary on midway through rolling so it gets pressed into the dough, gently stretching with your hands a little toward the end if necessary to get the dough to the right dimensions.

Heat a large cast-iron frying pan or griddle over medium-high heat until it's heated really well all the way through, 3 to 4 minutes. One at a time, pick up a piece of dough with a big metal spatula, lay it in the hot pan, cook for 1 minute or so until bubbles form, flip, cover and cook 1 more minute until darkened and bubbly. Remove from the pan, brush with melted butter, sprinkle with salt, and keep warm in a clean, folded kitchen towel while you make the other breads (if you can wait that long).

VEGETABLE NOODLES
with Parm & Basil

It's *so* nice to be able to bring some style to a pile of sadly lonely raw veg. All you have to do is get a vegetable peeler, and all of a sudden you're going all *Project Runway* on courgette. You just go *shk shk shk* and you have these ribbons that look *expensive*. You cook 'em for a minute, accessorize with olive oil, garlic and a snowstorm of Parm, and then it's: Courgette Noodles, you are the winner of this week's challenge. Regular noodles, you . . . are *out*.

SERVES 2 AS A MAIN DISH
OR 4 AS A SIDE DISH
ACTIVE TIME / 15 MIN
TOTAL TIME / 20 MIN

1 large courgette, ends trimmed, not peeled

1 large yellow squash or yellow courgette, ends trimmed, not peeled

6 asparagus spears, woody ends trimmed (see page 139)

1 large or 2 smaller carrots, peeled and trimmed

3 tablespoons olive oil, plus more for drizzling

4 cloves garlic, minced

½ teaspoon chilli flakes, or more to taste

Kosher salt and freshly ground black pepper

40 g finely grated Parmigiano-Reggiano cheese, plus more for garnish

Chopped fresh basil, for garnish

Place the courgette on a chopping board and hold it in place firmly. Using a vegetable peeler, apply pressure as you peel from one end of the courgette to the other to create 'noodles'. Peel until you hit seeds. Rotate the courgettes and repeat until you have all the nonseedy noodles you can get.

Repeat with the other vegetables. All of the noodles won't be the same thickness, and that's OK. Toss the vegetables together in a large bowl to mix them up a bit.

In a large frying pan, heat the oil over medium-high heat. Add the garlic and chilli flakes and cook until fragrant and the garlic is just starting to turn golden, 1 to 2 minutes. Add the vegetables and cook, tossing lightly but trying not to break them up, until they're just tender but not mushy, 3 to 4 minutes. Season with salt and black pepper, *generously* – look, you're basically just eating sautéed vegetables, so make 'em taste good.

Toss in the Parm and divide the noodles among bowls. Garnish with a drizzle of olive oil, a sprinkling of basil and more cheese.

Spicy Jammy
DRUMMIES

I dressed up these drummies with a shiny, sweet and spicy sauce and onions you drape over the tops like little scarves of goodness cloaking the chicken. They are pretty insanely delicious, and that is what I like to call . . . my jam.

SERVES 4
ACTIVE TIME / 25 MIN
TOTAL TIME / 1 HR 15 MIN

3 tablespoons rapeseed oil

2 large onions, thinly sliced

15 cloves garlic

325 g apricot or peach jam

1 teaspoon chilli flakes (we said *spicy*)

Kosher salt and freshly ground black pepper

8 chicken drumsticks (900 g to 1.2 kg total)

Preheat the oven to 425°F/220°C.

In a large heavy frying pan, heat the oil over medium-low heat. Add the onions and whole garlic cloves and cook, stirring often, until they soften and are light golden all the way through, about 20 minutes. Add the jam and chilli flakes and stir until the jam is melted, about 30 seconds. Season with salt and black pepper (season it on the light side because it's going to concentrate in the oven).

Transfer to a 23 × 33-cm baking dish (line it with foil if you like easy cleanup. Don't line it if you like to work for your clean pans). Season the drumsticks generously with salt and pepper, dump them on top of the onion-jam mixture, and spoon the onion stuff on top of the chicken to coat it. Bake until the mixture is bubbling, the chicken is cooked through with crisp skin, and the onions and garlic have darkened, 35 to 40 minutes, basting the chicken with the sauce every 15 minutes or so. If you want more colour, crank the grill on low and grill the chicken until the sauce bubbles and the onions darken, 1 to 2 minutes, but be careful not to burn it. Taste the sauce, season it with salt and pepper if necessary, and serve the drumsticks with the sauce drizzled on top.

SWEETS

Twitter's (and Uncle Mike's)
BANANA BREAD

Yes. This is THE banana bread. The bread that launched a million tweets and a hundred thousand Instagram tags, and had people all along the California coast offering to trade their brownest bananas for a makeup palette, a pair of John's used underwear (it was clean; I'm not an animal), and the chance to meet my trusty assistant/mom, @PepperThai2.

Perfecting this single recipe took me nearly a year. That's why I needed so many damn bananas. It was a fine, yummy banana bread. But something wasn't SPECIAL about it. I tried a million different things. Using banana pudding mix made it taste fake. Toasting the top with salty coconut made it a little too coconutty. Nuts were too controversial among my friends. Milk chocolate blended in too much. But! It turned out that putting the coconut *inside* left it with a subtle hint of sweet coconut goodness, vanilla pudding gave it a fluffy, moist texture I could never have imagined, and dark chocolate gave it a . . . I dunno, do I need to explain why putting in chocolate is a good thing? Can you toss nuts in this? Sure. Can you use a different chocolate? Why not. But I'm telling you – I did this every way humanly possible so you wouldn't have to. And the hundreds of banana bread pictures I'm tagged in (daily!) prove this.

And who is Uncle Mike, you ask? He's a guy who simply loves this bread. That was enough for me.

SERVES 12
ACTIVE TIME / 15 MIN
TOTAL TIME / 1 HR 15 MIN

6 mashed very ripe bananas*

4 eggs

170 ml rapeseed oil, plus a little more to grease the pan

250 g plain flour, plus a little more for dusting the pan

450 g sugar

1 (96-g) box vanilla instant pudding mix**

1 teaspoon baking soda

1½ teaspoons kosher salt

60 g unsweetened shredded coconut

1 (96-g) bar dark chocolate, chopped into chunks

Salted butter, for serving

Preheat the oven to 325°F/160°C.

In a large bowl, combine the mashed bananas, eggs and oil. In a separate bowl, combine the flour, sugar, pudding mix, baking soda and salt. Add the dry ingredients to the wet ingredients and combine well BUT GENTLY. I swear this came out differently when I used an aggressive electric mixer. Fold in the coconut and chocolate chunks.

Grease and flour a Bundt pan (that means wipe a little grease all over the inside of the pan, dust it with flour, and tip it upside down to shake out any extra flour). Pour the batter into the pan. (This can also make two 20 × 10-cm loaves, but it's so much more moist in one Bundt pan!)

Bake until the cake springs back when lightly pressed and a toothpick inserted into the centre comes out clean, 55 to 60 minutes. (Test it with a toothpick at around 50 minutes.) Let it cool slightly in the pan, then use a butter knife to gently release the cake from the sides of the pan and around the inner circle, then flip it on to a plate.

Let it cool and cut it into slices. Rewarm them and serve them with salty butter!!

★

Get six brown bananas. Not four. Not five. Six. You will think you only need five because it looks like enough, but it will not be enough. You will get five, you will mash them, you will be about half an inch short and that makes a difference and you cannot get around it. Trust me.

★ ★

I won't tell you what brand to use, but the right brand rhymes with smello. There's no exact equivalent in the UK, but it can easily be found online. Don't use banana-flavored pudding mix. I tried it. It is gross.

SOFT PRETZELS

Topped One, or Two, or Both Ways, or Not Topped at All, Why Not?

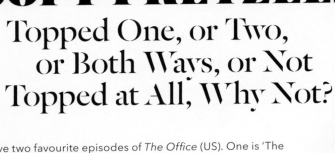

I have two favourite episodes of *The Office* (US). One is 'The Dinner Party', where Michael and Jan are that extremely awkward couple who fight the entire time and make everyone uncomfortable (believe it or not, John and I have been this couple before, but I did all the fighting). It is fantastic. Keep an eye out for the flat-screen TV scene. My other favourite episode is 'Pretzel Day' – Stanley and Michael *live* for pretzel day. Michael can't choose his favourite topping so he orders 'the works' and gets insanely hyper for the rest of the day. I feel him on a spiritual level with this one. Warm, soft, buttery pretzels are like a hug for your soul.

SERVES 6
ACTIVE TIME / 30 MIN
TOTAL TIME / 3 HRS

FOR THE PRETZELS

250 ml whole milk, at room temperature

1 packet instant or rapid-rise yeast (2¼ teaspoons)

3 tablespoons light brown sugar

1 tablespoon granulated sugar

435 g plain flour, plus more as needed

2½ teaspoons kosher salt

6 tablespoons butter, cut into pieces, at room temperature

750 ml hot tap water

50 g baking soda

FOR THE BUTTER AND CINNAMON SUGAR VERSION

110 g butter, melted

110 g granulated sugar

2 tablespoons ground cinnamon

¼ teaspoon kosher salt

FOR THE ICING VERSION

375 g icing sugar

125 ml whole milk

1 teaspoon vanilla extract

Finely grated zest of 1 small lemon

¼ teaspoon kosher salt

MAKE THE PRETZELS In a food processor fitted with the dough hook, mix together the milk, yeast, brown sugar and granulated sugar. Add the flour, 2 teaspoons of the salt and the butter and mix until the dough starts to come together, about 2 minutes. Increase the speed to medium and knead the dough for about 5 minutes, stopping the machine once in a while to pull down the dough if it climbs up the dough hook. Gather the dough into a ball, place it in a greased bowl, cover with plastic wrap, and let rise in a warm place until doubled in size, 1½ to 2 hours.

Preheat the oven to 425°F/220°C. Line two baking sheets with parchment paper.

In a shallow bowl or pie dish, stir together the hot water and baking soda and set aside.

Transfer the dough to a clean, lightly floured work surface and cut it into 6 equal pieces. Working with one piece of dough at a time (cover the rest with a kitchen towel to keep it from drying out), roll the piece of dough, working from the centre out, into a long rope about 60 cm long by 1 cm thick. Lift the ends of the dough to create a U-shape. Cross the dough arms twice, like the twisty part of a wire hanger, then lower the ends of the dough back down toward the bottom and press them slightly together to make them stick. (Or watch a YouTube video about shaping pretzels because let's be honest, that's probably wisest here. Or just shape them into whatever your fantasy of what a pretzel looks like and chill.)

Dip the pretzel into the baking soda bath (this gives it that pretzel shine) and place it on one of the baking sheets. Repeat with the remaining dough to form a total of 6 pretzels. Sprinkle the pretzels lightly with the remaining ½ teaspoon salt and bake, turning occasionally, until golden brown, 10 to 14 minutes. Transfer the pretzels (still on the parchment) to a rack to cool completely. Gently peel the pretzels from the parchment.

FOR THE BUTTER AND CINNAMON SUGAR VERSION Pour the melted butter into a shallow dish. In another shallow dish, mix together the granulated sugar, cinnamon, and salt. Dip each pretzel into the butter, then coat on both sides with the cinnamon sugar.

FOR THE ICING VERSION In a shallow bowl, combine the icing sugar, milk, vanilla, lemon zest and salt. Dip one side of each pretzel in the icing.

FOR THE COMBINATION VERSION Make the cinnamon sugar (omit the melted butter) and the icing. Dip one side of each pretzel in the icing and sprinkle with the cinnamon sugar.

SERVES 4 TO 6
ACTIVE TIME / 15 MIN
TOTAL TIME / 20 MIN

FRUIT SALAD
with Coconut-Lime Dressing

Oh, I cannot wait for the photos to flood in of this dish being a breakout star at your brunches or barbecues. I promise you, nooooooo one at your gathering has ever had a fruit salad like this one.

You could really pick any fresh fruit you'd like, but I feel like pineapple, lychee, mango and papaya make for a pretty epic fruit superhero grouping.

If you spoon this on top of some of the salty coconut rice from my first book, letting that dressing drizzle down to the bottom, I'll feel it no matter where you are or where I am. I will feel it. And we will both get pregnant.

60 g unsweetened shredded coconut

60 ml full-fat coconut milk, shaken

4 teaspoons light brown sugar

Grated zest of 1 lime

1 tablespoon fresh lime juice

⅛ teaspoon kosher salt

900 g mixed fruit (any combination of large chunks of pineapple, mango, papaya, kiwi, dragon fruit, canned lychees, etc.)

In a small heavy frying pan, toast the coconut over medium heat, stirring until golden and fragrant, about 4 minutes. Transfer it to a plate right away to cool – it might burn if you keep it in the pan!

In a large bowl, whisk together the coconut milk, brown sugar, lime zest, lime juice and salt.

Arrange the fruit on a serving platter, drizzle with the coconut dressing, and top with the toasted coconut.

Peanut Butter Chocolate Chip
BLONDIES

Hi guys. It's John here. Sometimes I hear that Chrissy and I are an iconic couple or #RelationshipGoals, but you should know that the *ultimate* couple has already been with us for years. They have weathered so many storms together. They have survived the bubonic plague and several Ebola scares. They are loved around the world. They are peanut butter and chocolate. Peanut butter and chocolate belong together and their love makes the world a tastier place. Chrissy made this dessert because she loves me and knows how much I love this magical combination. Thank you, Chrissy. You make life worth living.

Hey guys. Chrissy here. Just let John know that rats also survived the bubonic plague.

SERVES 10 TO 12
ACTIVE TIME / 10 MIN
TOTAL TIME / 1 HR

- 110 g butter, slightly softened, plus more for the skillet
- 170 g crunchy peanut butter
- 50 g light brown sugar
- 150 g granulated sugar
- 2 teaspoons vanilla extract
- 2 eggs
- 310 g flour
- 1 teaspoon kosher salt
- 1 teaspoon baking powder
- 140 g peanut butter chips (available online)
- 120 g chocolate chips (milk or dark)
- Vanilla ice cream, for serving

Preheat the oven to 350°F/180°C. Generously butter a 25-cm cast-iron frying pan.

In the bowl of a stand mixer fitted with the paddle attachment, beat together the butter, peanut butter, brown sugar and granulated sugar until creamy, scraping down the sides of the bowl if you need to, 1 to 2 minutes. Add the vanilla, then beat in the eggs one at a time, waiting until the first is incorporated before adding the second. In a small bowl, whisk together the flour, salt and baking powder. Turn off the mixer before adding the flour mixture, then beat until just combined. Mix in the peanut butter chips and chocolate chips.

Spread the batter into the pan and bake until the outside is a little golden on the edges but the centre is still soft and gooey, 40 to 45 minutes (it may seem undercooked when it comes out of the oven, but it firms up as it cools). Cool in the pan and cut into wedges or any shape you want. Serve warm with vanilla ice cream, or completely cooled.

Instant MANGO SORBET

This mango sorbet takes about as much time and energy as I am willing to put into making a frozen dessert at this point (read: almost zero time). Which is great, because literally all you have to do is cut some ripe juicy mangoes, freeze them (or better yet, just buy a bag of already frozen), and whir those fruit cubes with a few other things in a food processor until voilà, sorbet. YOU JUST MADE SORBET AND ALL YOU HAD TO DO WAS PUT FROZEN FRUIT IN A FOOD PROCESSOR. You don't have to tell anyone.

MAKES 500 ML SORBET;
SERVES . . . HOW MANY
PEOPLE DO YOU NEED
TO EAT HALF A LITRE OF
SORBET?
ACTIVE TIME / 10 MIN
TOTAL TIME / 4 HRS 10 MIN*

2 medium ripe mangoes, peeled and cubed (see Tip), or 450 g frozen mango chunks

3 tablespoons honey

125 ml full-fat coconut milk, shaken

Pinch of kosher salt

Arrange the mango cubes on a plate, cover tightly with plastic wrap and freeze until solid, at least 4 hours. You can keep the frozen mango in the freezer for up to 1 month.

In a bowl, whisk together the honey, coconut milk and salt. Combine the frozen mango and the honey mixture in a blender or food processer and process until smooth, stopping and scraping down the sides of the bowl if necessary, 1 to 2 minutes. Serve immediately, or freeze for 1 to 2 hours to harden. Sorbet can be kept in the freezer in an airtight container for up to 2 weeks; just remove from the freezer and let it soften up a bit, about 10 minutes, before serving.

★ / Total time is only **10 minutes** if you start with already-frozen mango!

Tip / *HOW TO PIT A MANGO*

Use a sharp peeler to peel off all the skin. Then stand the mango up on its long, thin side. Use a sharp knife to slice through the mango toward the centre, feeling for and cutting around the pit with the knife to release the mango flesh. Repeat with the other side, then use the knife to carve the rest of the mango flesh away from the pit.

Homemade 'MAGIC SHELL'

MAKES 450 ML
ACTIVE TIME / 2 MIN
TOTAL TIME / 10 MIN

Someday a long time from now, when I am on my deathbed after I have served this incredible dessert thousands of times and people have asked me over and over . . . *What is your secret, Chrissy-Wan? How do you make melted chocolate taste like coconuts and harden over ice cream in 30 seconds flat?* I will pull them in close and whisper into their ear . . . *It was the coconut oil, my young disciples.* That's the secret ingredient in this much-better-than-the-bottle version of your childhood fave.

230 g semisweet chocolate, chopped

185 ml coconut oil

Pinch of fine sea salt

In a microwave-safe bowl, combine the chocolate, coconut oil and salt and microwave in 15-second increments, stirring after each, until smooth, 45 seconds to 1 minute total. Let cool to room temperature. Serve on ice cream. Store in the refrigerator (it will harden up when it's cold) and gently melt for reuse.

Two-Faced
COBBLER

Pop Quiz: What's the difference between a cobbler, a buckle, a brown betty, a slump, a crisp, and a crumble? TBH I'm not really sure, so let's focus on what they have in common: You put fruit underneath them and bake until golden and toasty. Since kitchen decisions are never easy for me, I'm offering up two of these toppings – a biscuit-like cobbler and a, well, crumbly crumble – so you can half-and-half it all the way to dessert victory.

SERVES 10 TO 12
ACTIVE TIME / 45 MIN
TOTAL TIME / 2 HRS

Butter, for the pan

FOR THE FRUIT

2.2 kg nectarines, peaches, plums, or a combination (about 10 large or 15 medium pieces of fruit)

60 ml fresh lemon juice

2 tablespoons cornflour

75 g granulated sugar

½ teaspoon ground cinnamon

FOR THE COBBLER TOPPING*

125 g plain flour

110 g granulated sugar, plus more for sprinkling

1½ teaspoons baking powder

¼ teaspoon kosher salt

1 egg, beaten

5 tablespoons butter, very soft

FOR THE OAT TOPPING*

55 g old-fashioned rolled oats

110 g plain flour

75 g granulated sugar

50 g light brown sugar

55 g slivered almonds or chopped pecans or walnuts

1 teaspoon ground cinnamon

½ teaspoon kosher salt

110 g butter, slightly softened and cut into pieces

Vanilla ice cream or whipped cream, for serving

Preheat the oven to 350°F/180°C. Grease a 23 × 33 cm baking dish with butter.

PREPARE THE FRUIT Pit and slice the fruit into 1.5-cm wedges. In a large bowl, toss the fruit with the lemon juice, cornflour, granulated sugar and cinnamon. Transfer to the baking dish.

MAKE THE COBBLER TOPPING In a medium bowl, whisk together the flour, granulated sugar, baking powder and salt with a fork. With a spoon, stir in the egg and then the butter until incorporated (the dough will have the texture of soft cookie dough). Chill in the refrigerator for 15 minutes.

MAKE THE OAT TOPPING In another bowl, whisk together the oats, flour, granulated sugar, brown sugar, almonds, cinnamon and salt with a fork. Add the butter and pinch it in with your fingers until the topping is in smallish clumps.

Drop the cobbler topping in 2-tablespoon clumps over half the fruit filling (you will still see some fruit underneath; the dough won't cover it completely) and sprinkle the tops of the dough clumps with sugar. Scatter the oat topping over the other half of the fruit.

Bake until the juices are bubbling around the edges and both toppings are golden, about 1 hour. Remove from the oven and cool on a wire rack, about 20 minutes. Serve warm with vanilla ice cream or whipped cream.

 If you want to do just one topping, double the ingredient amounts for whichever one you choose.

Three-Ingredient CHOCOLATE MOUSSE with Salty Rice Krispies–Hazelnut Crackle

Have you ever noticed that like every restaurant that doesn't have an actual pastry chef (meaning someone whose only job it is to make desserts) always has mousse on the menu? Now I know why: Pretty much anyone can make it, and you can stash it in the fridge and top it with whipped cream and basically be the champion of the sweet things.

This version is even easier than usual because you don't have to whip egg whites (*plus* the Universe of Twittershame can't ride my butt about endangering the health of my children by eating raw eggs). It's just chocolate, milk and cream for the mousse – and the win. Bonus points if you load it into pretty glasses, though it tastes just as good in a paper cup. And you can make the crispy cereal candy toys that go on the top in ten minutes flat and they are insaaaaaanely good.

SERVES 4
ACTIVE TIME / 15 MIN
TOTAL TIME / 2 HRS 15 MIN

FOR THE MOUSSE
- **170 g good semisweet or dark chocolate chips or roughly chopped solid chocolate**
- **85 ml whole milk**
- **185 ml double cream**

FOR THE CRACKLE
- **Oil, for the pan**
- **150 g sugar**
- **4 teaspoons light corn syrup**
- **⅛ teaspoon baking soda**
- **¼ teaspoon kosher salt, plus more for sprinkling**
- **20 g Rice Krispies cereal**
- **60 g chopped toasted hazelnuts**

FOR SERVING
- **125 ml double cream**
- **1 tablespoon sugar**

MAKE THE MOUSSE In a large microwave-safe bowl, combine the chocolate chips and milk. Microwave on high for 1 minute 15 seconds. Remove and stir the mixture until melted and smooth; let it cool for 15 minutes.

Once the chocolate is cooled, whip the cream with a whisk or electric mixer until stiff peaks form (see Note), 2 to 3 minutes. Gently fold the whipped cream into the cooled chocolate until uniform, making sure not to stir too hard or the mousse will deflate. Divide evenly among four smallish glasses, like juice glasses or martini glasses (use them for something else for a change). Chill in the refrigerator for at least 2 hours or up to 24.

MAKE THE CRACKLE Line a baking sheet with parchment paper and grease lightly with oil. In a small (2-litre) saucepan, combine the sugar, 2 tablespoons water and the corn syrup. Bring to a boil over medium heat and let it bubble, swirling it occasionally, until the mixture turns toasty, the colour of nice caramel, about 5 minutes from when it starts to bubble. Remove the pot from the heat and stir in the baking soda and salt, then the Rice Krispies and hazelnuts. Working fast (the stuff hardens), spread the mixture on to the parchment and sprinkle with more salt. Let it cool and harden, then break into pieces.

ASSEMBLE THE MOUSSE With a whisk or electric mixer, whip the cream and the sugar to soft peaks. Top each glass of mousse with some of the whipped cream and the broken crackle.

Note / PEAKS

'Soft peak' cream means the cream holds nice shapes when lifted with a spoon or whisk, but the tips will still kinda flop over.

'Stiff peak' cream is prrrrrretty stiff: If you run a finger through the centre, there'll be a hollow channel there.

ACKNOWLEDGEMENTS

I am eternally grateful for the talented, patient and delightfully lovely humans who made this book possible.

It's easy to have passion and excitement for something, but it takes a small village to really make sure it all comes together. I've always joked that whenever I have a great idea, I write it into my palm and blow it away like a kiss into the sky because, let's face it, execution isn't my strong suit. So thank you to these people who have become my personal palm: to my coauthor, Adeena Sussman, for making sure every bite of cheese was just melty enough, every idea was indeed doable, and, more than anything, being there for me during the downs and eventual ups of postpartum life. We started this book in a difficult time and it was a trip to navigate at first, but your patience and love (of both me and food!) made this happen. I cannot wait for YOUR book! To my editor, Francis Lam, there is a reason everyone in the industry gushes about you. You are as funny and kind as you are brilliant and talented. You know more about food than any one human should but without being an asshole about it. It's really a special thing. I cannot wait to have 100 more books with you. To the INCREDIBLE team at Clarkson Potter – Aaron Wehner, Doris Cooper, Marysarah Quinn, Laura Palese, and everyone else – I could not have wished for a better publisher. You have never wanted to push out a book just for the sake of putting out a

'celebrity' cookbook. You genuinely care about authenticity and taste, the two things that are truly vital in the sea of cookbooks that are put out every year. Your excitement is contagious – I have endless love for you all.

To Mark Schulman and Luke at 3Arts, you make every dream happen. No one (besides Christine) puts up with more than you two. Thank you for both your business smarts and bellies and love and friendship.

To my loves at WME/IMG: Ivan Bart, Strand Conover, Jason Hodes, Meghan Mackenzie, Andy McNicol, Lisa Benson and Josh Otten, you guys are a force – the merger the world needed! Your belief in me from day one is never forgotten. I hope to continue to make you proud for a long time. Is that the world's first backhanded thank you? I love you guys.

To Britney Ross and Marisa Martins at 42West, my close girlfriends and literal lifesavers, true Smokey the Bears for the fires you've put out. Thank you for allowing me to have a life of keeping you on your toes, for all your much-needed advice, for making me laugh, and for talking me off ledges. I really, really love and appreciate you both.

To my team at DSMTFL: Nina Shaw, you are why they came up with the term #goals. Strong, powerful, smart, savvy – I don't trust a move I make without your input. Laurie Megery and Abel Lezcano, thank you for being such a huge part of a huge year. I appreciate you all.

To David Levin, quite possibly the only ex-male model, romance novel cover star turned business manager in the world, you have been a best friend since the day I met John. Thank you for the endless support, the delicious dinners at Carbone, the white suits and the constant entertainment of stopping my friends dead in their tracks: 'Who IS that handsome man!?' I trust you with my life. Love you and your family. To Melissa Konstantatos, thank you for keeping our man together and being so on top of every move made!

To my photo team and food stylists: Aubrie Pick, Cortney Munna, Bessma Khalaf, Sandra Garcia, Fanny Pan, Elizabeth Normoyle, Kristene Loayza, Kira Corbin and Leah Rom – it is safe to say this book would be nothing without you. Thank you to your eyes, your hands, for making this book beautiful, and for being so ridiculously easy to work with. I love the story you've told through pictures and cannot wait for the world to see.

To my squad! Mary Phillips, Kristine Studden, Patrick Ta, Carly Fisher, Laura Polko, Jen Atkin, Monica Rose, Alana Van Deraa, Katie Peare, Dave Thomas, Matteo Pieri – thank you for making me look and feel pretty. There is no other way to say it. You are the true dream team. I feel very lucky to have been able to find people that are not only talented as F but are truly, truly good people to the core.

To my friend and assistant, Christine Shim, who put together this list of people to thank but did not include herself – thank you for being the driver of this bus, the only reason I make any deadlines, answer any emails, get to any job, make any flight. The amount of random shit you have to do on a daily basis is astounding and you do it all without breaking a sweat or choking me out. I love you. Thank you for being so good to me and my family.

To Mom, Dad and Tina, I owe my life to you. I love you.

To Pippa, Penny, and Paul – thank you for being my vacuums. You are good dogs, most of the time. You sleep the rest of the time. But I love you.

To my Puddy in doggy heaven, our first born pup: I think about you every day. We will miss you always. John won't let me name baby boy after you. Just know I tried.

This book is for the loves of my life: John, Luna and baby boy. Thank you for the incredible life you have given me. I am truly the luckiest girl in the world.

INDEX

MICHAEL JOSEPH

UK | USA | Canada | Ireland | Australia
India | New Zealand | South Africa

Michael Joseph is part of the Penguin Random House
group of companies whose addresses can be found at
global.penguinrandomhouse.com

Penguin
Random House
UK

First published in the United States by Clarkson Potter/
Publishers, an imprint of the Crown Publishing Group, a
division of Penguin Random House LLC, New York, 2018
First published in the United Kingdom by Michael Joseph 2018
001

Copyright © Chrissy Teigen, 2018
Photographs copyright © Aubrie Pick, 2018

The moral right of the author has been asserted

Printed in Italy by L.E.G.O. S.p.a.

A CIP catalogue record for this book is available from the
British Library

HARDBACK ISBN: 978-0-718-18798-9

www.greenpenguin.co.uk

MIX
Paper from
responsible sources
FSC® C018179

Penguin Random House is committed to a
sustainable future for our business, our readers
and our planet. This book is made from Forest
Stewardship Council® certified paper.

Banana Bundt Bread

* key flavors: banana, vanilla pudding, dark chocolate,

2 cups mashed BROWN bananas
4 eggs
2/3 cup canola oil (plus a little more to grease the
2 cups flour (plus a little more to flour the pan)
2 cups sugar
1 box of vanilla instant pudding (box is 3.5oz)
1 teaspoon baking soda
1 teaspoon salt
1 cup unsweetened shredded coconut
3.5oz bar of dark chocolate or I dunno a ½ cup dar
chocolate chips (can add more if you love dark ch

combine mashed bananas, eggs & oil in a large bowl. In a
different large bowl, combine the flour, sugar, pudding
baking soda and salt. add dry ingredients to the wet ing
bowl and combine

fold in coconut and chocolate chunks. pour into greased
floured bundt pan (this can also make 2 loaves but it's
so much better/moist to me in one bundt pan!)

serve warmed up slices with sweet salty butter chunk
(Irish butter mu

Bake at 3
(too
skewer or toothpick around 50 min. let
lightly, flip onto another plate! (use a butter knif
gently release from pan before flipping. don't forget
inner circle!)